SACRED
ENCOUNTERS
with Mary

SACRED ENCOUNTERS
with Mary

G. Scott Sparrow, Ed.D.

ThomasMore®
– An RCL Company –
Allen, Texas

NIHIL OBSTAT:
Rev. Msgr. Glenn D. Gardner, J.C.D.
Censor Librorum

IMPRIMATUR:
† Most Rev. Charles V. Grahmann
Bishop of Dallas

May 15, 2002

The Nihil Obstat and Imprimatur are official declarations that the material
reviewed is free of doctrinal or moral error. No implication is contained therein that
those granting the Nihil Obstat and Imprimatur agree with the contents, opinions,
or statements expressed.

Acknowledgment
The Scripture quotations contained herein are from the *New Revised Standard Version
Bible: Catholic Edition* copyright © 1993 and 1989 by the Division of Christian
Education for the National Council of the Churches of Christ in the U.S.A. Used by
permission. All rights reserved.

Send all inquiries to:
Thomas More® Publishing
An RCL Company
200 East Bethany Drive
Allen, Texas 75002-3804

Telephone: 800-264-0368 / 972-390-6300
Fax: 800-688-8356 / 972-390-6560

Visit us at: **www.thomasmore.com**
Customer Service E-mail: **cservice@rcl-enterprises.com**

Printed in the United States of America

7489   ISBN 0-88347-489-1

1 2 3 4 5   06 05 04 03 02

*F*or Kathy,
who knows
Mary as a
friend

"ONE OF THE MOST MISUNDERSTOOD AND LOVELY elements of Catholicism, both Roman and Orthodox, is the spirituality which centers around Mary, the mother of Jesus. This book grows out of Scott Sparrow's heart and the spiritual passion of his heart, which is devoted to Mary. . . . In his own and others' mystical encounters with Mary, he consistently emphasizes the relationship Mary cultivates with the believer, which in turn complements and points to the believer's relationship with Jesus. 'Miraculous appearances and phenomena, even instances of spontaneous healing, are treated as elements in service of a trusting and loving relationship with Mary and Jesus.'

"Sacred Encounters with Mary serves as a kind of practical spiritual handbook that addresses the problems of suffering, spiritual surrender, holiness, and spiritual discipline. The most wonderful thing about this book, however, is that it simply rings true. The experience of God is hard to talk about or write about, but you know it when you encounter it. This is not a book about God or about Mary; it is a work of love from a man of faith, and this is why it inspires a response like that of the mother of Jesus: a simple and sincere 'yes.' "

Tom Baker
Counselor and lecturer,
Virginia Beach, VA

Contents

Foreword

WHEN ONE CONSIDERS THE VIOLENCE AND RACIAL animosity that prevails in many areas of the world today, it is easy to become discouraged. And yet, in my work as a spiritual healer and teacher, I have witnessed countless examples of the Spirit working through prayer to heal people of crippling disabilities, "terminal" illnesses and mental disorders. All of this points to an obvious conclusion—that God manifests his great love and mercy even in the most troubled times.

If all of these wondrous events were not enough to convince us of God's presence among us, the widespread apparitions of the Blessed Virgin Mary should dispel our remaining doubts. Even so, there was a time when I looked upon Mary's manifestations with skepticism. Through a series of pilgrimages to the site of the most famous current apparition of the Blessed Virgin, my skepticism dissolved, and my life began anew.

It all began in 1985. By then, I had already been involved with spiritual healing work for ten years, yet I was quite aware that something was missing from my life. While I had witnessed many people being healed or cured instantly from various maladies, it seemed to me that my life was disintegrating more and more into a slump—a dark night of the soul, if you will.

Around this time, my associate in the healing work, Paul Funfsinn, traveled to the tiny village of Medjugorje in the country of Bosnia, a part of the former Yugoslavia. Upon his return, he shared with me his incredible experiences of supernatural phenomena surrounding the apparitions of the Blessed Virgin Mary that were reportedly taking place there.

At that time, I was still a Roman Catholic priest pastoring a small country parish. Even so, I found it hard to believe in such things as apparitions, although the spiritual healing in which I was involved could be considered a similar "spiritual phenomenon." Paul decided he wanted to return to Medjugorje, and he wanted me to go, too.

After much persuasion, I decided to go along but for only one purpose: I wanted to know and fulfill God's will for me. In other words, it was not my purpose to go and be caught up in what I termed a "spiritual high." Without knowing it, however, I was in for a profound and unsettling awakening.

Indeed, going to Medjugorje had traumatic and dramatic effects on my life. It was traumatic because I discovered through Mary's intervention that I lacked sufficient love to be serving Jesus adequately. The experience was dramatic because it ushered me into a transitional stage in my spiritual journey through which I was eventually empowered to serve others more completely than ever before. Looking back, I now realize that my visits to Medjugorje prepared me to make a deeper commitment to the God I already claimed to serve.

We arrived in Medjugorje on a weekday, and immediately I could sense that this indeed was an extraordinary place in the spiritual sense of the word. On the surface, however, it was your typical East European "poor" village.

As I was roaming around near the Church of St. James, a Catholic nun who worked with the visionaries—those who were said to be seeing Mary—approached me and invited me to join a small group that would be with the visionaries at the time of Mary's apparition. "Indeed, yes!" I responded.

My awakening was about to begin. Entering the room with the others, we each found a spot where we could be comfortable. The "apparition room" was a tiny "cell" in the home of the Franciscan priests who were serving the parish. The visionaries, along with one of the priests and the nun, entered the room. I did not know then that a bright light typically precedes the apparition or that the visionaries would literally fall to the floor on their knees when Mary appeared. Quite honestly, I really did not know what to expect. When the light appeared like a bolt of lightning, however, it knocked me off my knees and "threw" me against the wall!

I was afraid to open my eyes, believing people were staring at me. When I was able to muster the courage and open my eyes, no one was paying any attention to me. In fact, their focus was upon God, to whom they were praying. At the end of the session I left the room bewildered, unaware as yet that what had just occurred was about to transform me and my work forever.

Over the next few days, I had several deeply moving, extraordinary experiences. The chain of my new crystal rosary, purchased prior to my departure, turned gold—a "normal" phenomenon among the many visitors to Medjugorje, I was later informed. In the room where priests were allowed to celebrate Mass for the people coming to Medjugorje, the image of Christ suddenly appeared on a statue of Mary. My associate was able to capture the phenomenon on film. After he snapped the picture, the image disappeared.

We were able to stare at the sun without hurting our eyes. It danced and pulsated and was overlaid with what appeared to be a large whole-wheat wafer—like a communion host. On the left of this image was the kneeling figure of the Blessed Virgin.

This was only my first trip to Medjugorje and I was given so much to digest. My second trip occurred only six months later. Between 1985 and 1988, I was prompted to make four trips to this remarkable sacred site. I guess I am a slow learner!

During the course of the other three trips, astounding things continued to happen. The chain of another rosary, which I had owned for a long time, turned gold. I witnessed more "light phenomena" in Medjugorje; and, upon returning home, I saw the sun spinning over my own parish in Illinois one evening prior to a healing service. Some fifty attendees witnessed this supernatural event with me.

I could go on and on, but these experiences in themselves do not change or transform one's life unless they are pondered prayerfully. In so doing, we allow the Holy Spirit to reveal the underlying truth of these events. My main purpose for going to Medjugorje was to seek God's will for my life. After much meditating on the events which accompanied my journeys to this isolated village, some deeply disturbing revelations were given to me which would enhance the course of my life thereafter.

For instance, I was informed by an inner voice that I had been too "hard" in dealing with people who were sick and in need of help. Although the power and the healing was God's Spirit, my lack of compassion was closing the channel for me to experience the same joy people were feeling through their communion with God.

I was also told that I lacked the quality of the feminine energy of God—that is, tenderness and mercy—which Mary, the Mother of Jesus, symbolized. In other words, Mary could be viewed as the feminine aspect of God, or the feminine archetype of God.

This tenderness and mercy was evidently missing from my healing work. There was no doubt in my mind that these revelations were a true characterization of what I had become. I had been so busy with the work of the Lord that I had forgotten the Lord of the work.

I eventually realized that as I meditated more on Jesus, Mary, the Holy Spirit, and the Christ consciousness, God could mold me into an embodiment of love, mercy, tenderness, strength, and power. Recognizing God as a God of love enabled me to rise above the seeming tragedies of life into the very heart of the mother-and-father-God that Jesus himself knew.

I came to see that Mary and Jesus, taken together, express the completeness of both the masculine and the feminine energy found in the "personality" of God. These events and revelations have empowered my personal life and healing work in a profoundly moving way. I am now able, through the Holy Spirit, to be a clearer channel for God's presence and power and to introduce others to their God—a Being not only of power, but of tenderness, care and mercy.

In the gospel of Saint Luke, a legalist approaches Jesus seeking the answer to life itself. Jesus then asks him to interpret the greatest commandment. The legalist quotes the words, "You shall love the Lord your God and your neighbor as yourself." Jesus then says, "Do this and you will live." Similarly, God's message through Mary remains: Love God in one another and his peace will radiate from humanity's heart.

This is what it is all about. All other phenomena, including encounters with Mary and Jesus, serve only one purpose—to call us to return to our true natures, and to love and to experience life fully. In all of her manifestations, Mary tells how this can be accomplished—through authentic prayer from the heart.

Mary, the tender mother of Jesus, is also our mother. She is the mother of mercy and the companion of all, regardless of one's religion or the lack thereof. No religion can claim to have a monopoly on Mary's motherly love: Mary is for all of us. To embrace her is to become a humble servant of the Master. To be in communion with her is to experience the unparalleled empowerment that comes from saying "Yes" to God.

This book is a marvelous read, and it is clearly a gift to her and from her. It is my prayer that as you encounter Mary in the life-changing experiences included herein, you, too, will experience the spirit of Mary—her humility, her strength, her courage, and her call to each of us to put love above everything else.

Ron Roth
Celebrating Life
www.ronroth.com
LaSalle, Illinois

Introduction

SEVERAL YEARS AGO, A CLIENT OF MINE WAS approaching the end of her psychotherapeutic work with me. Through intensive individual and group therapy, she had resolved many wounds, including the trauma of having been raped by someone she had loved and trusted, and the corrosive effect of having been married to an alcoholic for twenty-seven years. She had begun bringing me parting gifts that were symbolic of our work together, such as a woolen prayer shawl that she had obtained years before on a pilgrimage to India. But the greatest gift of all was a vision that she shared with me tearfully during one of our last hours together. It was her third encounter with Mary, the mother of Jesus, and it ushered her through the last stage of her recovery into the light of a new day. The first part of Rachel's vision is as follows:

> *I am pulled awake—drawn out of a deep sleep. I see a little star through my bedroom window. I say silently, "Did you wake me?" I am loving this little star and thanking it for waking me up to enjoy the stillness of the night.*
>
> *I am aware that the star seems to be growing—getting wider. I reach for my glasses to make sure that I am really seeing this. I realize that I am seeing the moon, not a star,*

and that it is a new moon, like a rocking chair. So now I am loving this moon. The moon moves and seems to break up. It becomes two moons, with a second one to the right and below the first one. I shake my head to be sure, once again, that I am really seeing this. Then the moon on the right pulsates and expands into an orb—a brilliant, beautiful golden-white and silvery orb that becomes brighter and brighter. But it does not hurt my eyes even though it is more brilliant than a noonday sun.

I sit up to see better, and I am aware that everything in my room is also glowing and brilliant. I think at first that I must be dreaming, but then again I know that I am awake. I remember that I was reading your book[1] before I went to sleep, and the last thing I said before I went to sleep was, "Yes, she was indeed blessed, and so are you for having written this book for her and for all of us who have come to love her." I whispered "Thank you" to both of you.

Then a huge shaft of light streams down from the orb and right into my chest! I'm surprised and so happy, and I'm afraid to move, thinking that if I move I'll lose it. And, whatever it is, I want it to stay. My eyes must be as wide as saucers, and I'm saying, prayerfully, "Thank you, thank you, thank you." I don't move for a good while. I am aware that I am surrounded by my dear ones—beings, angels that have been with me for as long as I can remember. And you are with me, too, as you often have been in the last couple of years.

I am feeling loved and supported by your presence, and unafraid. I am then aware of colors in the shaft of light, and that I can move in my bed without losing the connection with the light. I am giddy with love and joy. The colors are blue and green and gold and yellow—all within a silver-white shaft of light. I marvel at this demonstration of the truth that all colors come together to make the white light. I say, "It's true!" I am in such joy, completely relaxed, and in no pain.[2] *I'm breathing gently, saying again, "Thank you, thank you."*

Then the shaft of light says, "You used to wear white."

I say, "Yes."

Then the light says, "Wear white again. It is all the colors. Wear white a lot."

The voice is very beautiful, very familiar and so gentle and loving. I am crying with tears streaming down my face, but it doesn't seem to matter. I get out of bed and move around the room. I'm laughing and crying and marveling at the sight and the sheer joy I feel!

I get back in bed and sit cross-legged, and I hear the sound. First, I hear a big bell—bong, bong, bong. Then it gets softer as if from a distance, but it is still deep and clear. Then I hear the lovely, indescribable sounds of "crystal" bells as they seem to tumble and tinkle—as if tumbling down a hill, along the gently rushing water, over rocks and stones. And then comes the sound of wind! And just as the white light is comprised of all the colors, I experience that the great sound contains all the sounds—the big bell, the small tinkling bells, the water, the wind, the music. The sound is also the One—the One I cannot describe, but I know it already in my head and heart. It reminds me of a place I've been before—not on earth, but I don't know where.

Once I hear the great sound, the One, my attention is completely steady. There is no wavering, no "brain talk." There is just the One, and it is sound and light and colors and love; and it is truly indescribable. Once I am immersed in the sound, I am "caught up" in it for some time.

Then the orb above me becomes larger, and a girl comes floating down on a shaft of light.

I think it must be Mary, yet she is so young, maybe fifteen or sixteen. As I reach out to her, I notice that my hands are young again. The girl and I are the same age, growing into womanhood. Yet we are still children who, it seems, have had to grow up quickly.

I hear her say clearly, as if it is the most natural thing in the world for us to talk together:

"This is what you have been searching for . . ."[3]

Rachel's experience is what we have *all* been searching for, whether we acknowledge it or not—an experience of a vast, encompassing love that will sustain us regardless of what happens in our lives. While this experience of divine presence can come in many forms, personal encounters with Mary, the mother of Jesus, seem to be increasing even more today than when she began appearing during times of upheaval to unlikely visionaries on hillsides and in other rural areas of Mexico and Europe. Indeed, it is often the feminine face of God that shines through and consoles us in times of our deepest personal and collective need.

Some say that Mary brings to us an awareness that we desperately need at this time—a nourishing spirit of self-sacrificing love that might, if embraced more widely, help to reverse the tide of hatred and bloodshed that is spilling into many regions of the world today, including our own. In support of this idea, one can point to the timing of the major apparitions: They almost always precede, or coincide with, regional or worldwide upheavals, and unprecedented opportunities. As author Janice Connell says, "When the Blessed Mother appears, great things happen on earth and in heaven."[4]

An old friend of mine, who was a member of a women's group devoted to the Blessed Mother, once had a vision of Mary in meditation. She saw the Blessed Mother as a nurturing, protective presence enveloping the earth:

In October 1988, I opened my meditation with a prayer to Mother Mary to bless the children of the earth. I then had a vision of the Divine Mother. I saw her as a deep blue mass moving over the face of the earth. I saw her reaching out with silvery-blue cords of energy, and knew that these were touching children—the innocent and vulnerable ones of the world whose lives were being sacrificed at the expense of the self-centered consciousness and destructive activities of mankind. Then I heard the words, "Children seven years 'fore and seven years hence." I understood that the arms of the Mother were protecting the children of the world who are at the mercy of abusive situations—politically or environmentally or parentally. I also saw that her protection extended to aspects of the world's threatened ecology. I experienced her presence for most of the day afterward, and I felt an immense sadness and compassion. (C.N.)

C.N.'s vision effectively captures the spirit of love—as well as the sense of urgency and warning—that has come to represent the Blessed Mother's influence on people today. Her vision also portrays the Blessed Mother as a world-encompassing force of love that reaches into the lives of innumerable people at this very moment, blending with and expressing herself through the diverse religious and mythical forms through which the world has come to know her.

Some of the Blessed Mother's most recent messages, through the various visionaries who have disseminated them, contain warnings that may seem incongruent with the popular conception of Mary as a messenger as divine love. But Mary does not typically appear to people who live in relative comfort, safely removed from the chaos of regional wars and political reprisals. To the contrary, she usually manifests in areas of religious and social instability, and her messages draw our attention to the tragedies unfolding in these places, and to the remedies that we ourselves can provide, especially through devotional practice. She reminds us of the grief that she carries for children who have no one else to care for them, and for those who are bereft of hope and faith. We cannot turn to her without waking up to much of what we'd rather forget is going on in this world. Mary calls upon us to deal now with the ways things are, not merely to dream about the way we would like them to be; and she points the way through these troubled times to the glorious promise of new beginnings.

Mary's consistently stated intent is to prepare us for Christ's coming—or the interior spiritual equivalent thereof. She tells us that unless we engage in more diligent spiritual practice, we may succumb to the trials and turmoil that might precede Christ's reappearance, or his Spirit's heightened influence within us. Along these lines, some say that Mary models for us the ideal human response to the Divine: Through emulating her, we can enter into a dynamic relationship with Christ, carrying his purpose to fruition in our lives much in the way that she graciously consented to her role in the conception and birth of Jesus. In this vein, three hundred years ago, Louis de Montfort, author of *True Devotion to Mary*, prophesied that Mary's manifestations not only would be important, but would necessarily precede the second coming of Christ:

> *In the second coming of Jesus Christ, Mary has to be made known and revealed by the Holy Spirit in order that, through her, Jesus Christ may be known, loved and served.*[5]

While one might accept the validity of Mary's contemporary manifestations—and the truth of messages that she has disseminated through those who have seen her—it is another thing altogether to experience the profound presence that the visionaries report. Most believers remain on the periphery of such events, deriving faith and hope from a vicarious participation in the visionaries' experience of Mary's presence. While the apparitions appear to only a few, many who have visited the apparition sites can feel her presence, even years later. In making pilgrimages to these places, believers and nonbelievers alike may undergo healings, or experience other inexplicable events that exert lasting effects on their lives. Although most of us remain blind to what the visionaries see, and removed from the ecstasy they have felt, the moving stories of their encounters, and the palpable presence that surrounds the apparition sites, convey a faith-awakening essence that the Blessed Mother clearly intends for us to experience, as well.

In the following pages, you will read many accounts of those who have *directly experienced* a presence whom they believe was Mary, the mother of Jesus. As one might expect, the majority of the recipients were raised Roman Catholic, but many of them had ceased to worship as Catholics when Mary manifested to them. Others, such as myself, are non-Catholics who became open to the Holy Mother through their own spiritual journey. Regardless of their current religious affiliations, many of the recipients have expressed a broad appreciation for other spiritual traditions.

Just as the historic apparitions have brought Mary out of the church into the lives of ordinary people, the accounts in this book will demonstrate compellingly that the phenomenon of the Blessed Mother's presence is becoming increasingly widespread and more personal—extending far beyond the doctrinal boundaries of the established churches and into the dreams and visions of individuals everywhere. Consequently, the reader—regardless of prior religious persuasion—may find himself or herself more ready and open to have an experience that once seemed beyond the reach of most seekers.

The Importance of Having a Relationship with Mary

In virtually every modern apparition, the visionaries typically receive and disseminate a brief message from Mary after every appearance. In contrast, most of the encounters that we will consider in this book reveal a Mary who remains silent or utters only a few memorable words. Indeed, some readers may puzzle at the contrast between the relatively quiet encounters in this book and the lengthy messages that have been reported elsewhere.

Mary's messages give us something that we can immediately understand and use to direct our lives. Yet, well-respected authorities have noted that even the most widely accepted messages from Mary—those derived from the major historic apparitions—"merely" reiterate the enduring spiritual truths espoused by Jesus and other scriptural sources.[6] If the message is so familiar, then why do they inspire so many people? I believe that *we respond to her messages not because the information is new, but because they draw us into a relationship with her.* Certainly, Mary's messages clarify the intent of the being who manifests to the visionaries; but a *relationship* with her is, perhaps, a far greater treasure for us to contemplate and to seek for ourselves. For, in knowing and relating to her ourselves, we can come to feel her promptings: We can learn what God might require of us, and how a relationship with the Blessed Mother might transform our lives. Through this inquiry, we might ourselves enjoy an enhanced capacity to commune directly with Mary.

How the Accounts Were Obtained and Treated

For the purposes of this book, I have defined a Marian encounter as any experience in which a person encounters directly the presence of a being whom they identify as Mary, the mother of Jesus. Most of the experiences included in the following chapters occurred as waking visions during meditation or prayer, in vivid dreams, or during apparent out-of-body experiences. A few were "locutions," in which Mary manifested to the recipient as a clear, inner voice.

The accounts were obtained from several different sources.

First, a couple of the contributors—such as Rachel—were my counseling clients, whose therapeutic work opened them to experiences of divine presence. Others responded to word-of-mouth notices and newspaper articles announcing this project, or to a magazine article that was published about my work.[7] And a few contributors answered an invitation that was included in the back of my first nationally published book.[8]

Understandably, most recipients of encounters with Christ or Mary are interested in preserving their privacy in order to avoid the kind of scrutiny and judgment that such experiences sometimes provoke in unsympathetic listeners: These experiences are simply too sacred to risk exposing them to ridicule. To respect the privacy of the contributors, therefore, I have identified them with only their initials.

The Common Theme of Love

In researching encounters with Mary and Jesus, I found to my amazement that one can summarize the experience of meeting them face-to-face with a single word—*love.* The love they reveal to those who witness their presence is vast and unconditional. Their love encompasses a complete knowledge of the person's history—including strengths, weaknesses, and otherwise "unredeemable" characteristics and behaviors. In such encounters, they rarely offer advice and hardly ever express any judgment toward the witness. Their messages are typically brief if they speak at all. Indeed, they usually remain silent except in regard to the "bigger" issues in life, such as loving more and serving more. Concerning these larger matters, they remain firmly and lovingly uncompromising, as one might expect. But they almost always leave the person with the twofold experience of being *completely known* and *completely loved.* This experience, in turn, affects each person in different ways, depending on what he or she needs at the time. Sometimes, physical healing follows the manifestation, sometimes a sense of emotional healing, and sometimes a realization of having been taught something profound and life changing.

To assist you in appreciating the dimensions of the Marian encounter, I have grouped the encounters according to discernible themes that unfold in the course of the experience. In addition, I have ventured a perspective on the aim or purpose that the encounter serves in the recipient's life. While this approach runs the risk of overly inserting my own views, I believe it may help you examine the deeper purpose and practical relevance of such spiritual encounters.

Who Is It, Really?

The question, Is it *really* Mary? will occur even to the most ardent believers as they read these accounts. For some, it will be hard to believe that these experiences have anything to do with a woman who lived and died two thousand years ago. It is difficult enough for some of us to accept that Jesus appears to individuals today, but at least his promises to manifest himself are clearly stated and reiterated in the Gospel of John:

"I will not leave you orphaned; I am coming to you. . . . They who have my commandments and keep them are those who love me; and those who love me will be loved by my Father, and I will love them and reveal myself to them" (John 14:18, 21).

Clearly, the Scriptures do not lay the same foundation for an ongoing relationship with Mary. She remained largely silent in the scriptural record: She made no promises to commune with us and left us very little through which we can know her as she was then. For better or worse, we must come to know the woman who was "the first of the believers of the new covenant"[9] through the growing body of experiences with her, including—if we are so fortunate— our own. Instead of seeing this as limiting, we might regard it as an opportunity to embark on a personal quest to behold the Blessed Mother through our own experiences. Given the abundant devotional writings about Mary over the course of Christianity's history, and her availability as a spiritual presence, we can see that Mary is as knowable as the heart is open to her. Of course, any private spiritual experience bears the imprint of the visionary's cultural heritage, beliefs, and expectations; and one cannot easily subtract out these conditioning factors from the encounter. The Holy Mother does not seem to hold this against us, and seems willing to adapt her appearance to the person and context of her manifestation.

For instance, when the archangel Michael appeared to the four girls in Garabandal, Spain, he eventually announced that Mary would appear to them as our Lady of Mount Carmel—one of many familiar ways that Mary has been depicted in the Catholic tradition. In essence, the angel implied that the form of Mary's appearance was only one of many possible ways that she could manifest to them. Another apparition of Mary appeared over a period of several years to a group of young people in the St. Maria Goretti Church in

Scottsdale, Arizona. When she manifested, she appeared to several young people at the same time; but *she appeared differently to each one.*[10] As Father Robert Faricy observed:

> *In each of her comings, Mary appears in such a way that the people to whom she comes can relate to her. To black people she is black. To Koreans she looks Korean. . . . She comes as their Mother because that is what she is. Ours, too.*[11]

Rather than considering the individual variations as distortions, we can treat the myriad of ways in which individuals experience the Blessed Mother as partial but invaluable information about a being who, ultimately, can *only* be known through the eyes and hearts of human visionaries, anyway.

With this in mind, let us consider the notion that by appreciating the various forms in which the Blessed Mother manifests to us, we may enter more deeply into a personal relationship with God, and gain knowledge of the unifying spirit that expresses itself in a myriad of forms. By suspending our need to separate subjective from objective—and by *feeling* its presence—we may draw closer than ever to the grace-filled being who impels us onward, and forever assists us on our journey.

In practice, as Garabandal scholar Father J. I. Pelletier says, "The degree of our devotion to Mary will be a matter of discerning the authentic promptings of the Holy Spirit. The same Spirit will attract some to honor and pray to angels, others to this or that saint. So, too, it is in regard to Mary."[12] But, as he goes on to say, "We must not be afraid of loving Mary too much." C. S. Lewis agreed that it is far more important to worship God in whatever form appeals to us than it is to be offended by its degree of personhood. As he once wrote, "What soul has ever perished by believing that God the Father has a beard?"[13]

Or, for that matter, a mother's touch.

OUR LADY
of Guadalupe

"Am I not here with you, who am your Mother?
Is there anything else that you need?"

Our Lady of Guadalupe to Juan Diego, 1531

IN 1531, ONLY TEN YEARS AFTER THE SPANISH conquest of Mexico, Mary appeared to a newly converted Aztec Indian, Juan Diego, as he was walking to Mexico City to receive Christian instruction. There on the barren hillside above the city, he encountered a beautiful lady who introduced herself as the Virgin Mary, and told him that she wanted a church built there so pilgrims could come there and worship. Juan immediately took this message to the bishop, and was turned away for obvious reasons. On his way back, Juan encountered Mary again, who convinced him to go back and try again the next day. Even though Juan could not figure out why she had chosen him, a lowly peasant, he agreed to try once more.

Impressed with his sincerity, the bishop told Juan that he needed some proof that he wasn't making it all up. When Juan went back and told Mary what the bishop had said, she asked him to return the following day to receive the proof that the bishop requested. But the next day, Juan's uncle became terribly ill, and so he went in search of help for his ailing uncle. Hoping that the Lady would forgive him for missing the appointment, he took a path around the mountain, hoping to avoid her. But Mary stood in his way, and had other plans for him. After assuring him that his uncle would recover, Mary told Juan to go pick some of the dew-covered roses that were miraculously growing on the mountaintop in the midwinter cold. When he returned to the path below, he found Mary waiting. She then helped him arrange the roses inside his crude overcoat, or *tilma,* and sent him into Mexico City to visit the bishop, once again.

When Juan spread his *tilma* and the roses at the feet of the bishop and a visitor—who just so happened to be the new governor of Mexico—they witnessed an even greater miracle than fresh roses in winter. On the inside of his garment, they beheld a beautiful painting that depicted the Blessed Mother in prayer. They fell to their knees before her image and were convinced, finally, that our Lady had appeared to Juan. Her request was fulfilled, and a magnificent cathedral stands today on the spot where our Lady of Guadalupe first appeared to him. It enshrines the painting that Juan received over 450 years ago.

1

THE CHILDHOOD
Encounter

*"O Ark of the New Covenant, clad on all sides
with purity in place of gold; the one in whom
is found the Golden vase with its true manna,
that is the flesh in which lies the God-head."*

From a sermon on Mary by
Athanasius of Alexandria (295–373)[14]

WHEN I FIRST BEGAN MY RESEARCH ON MARIAN
visions and dreams, I felt obliged to explore the roots of devotion to
Mary in the early church. I read about the different beliefs and
religious debates about her nature and her role in the redemptive
process, and I immersed myself in the imagery that grew out of
centuries of veneration to her. In particular, I was intrigued to
discover how early Christians drew comparisons between Mary
and the Ark of the Covenant—even to the point of referring to Mary
as *the Ark of the New Covenant* since she carried God's new

covenant within her womb. Along these lines, the visionary nun Catherine Emmerich, who lived in Germany in the early 1800s, observed in one of her many visions that Mary's conception involved a transmission of a luminous, most secret presence from the Ark of the Covenant into the womb of Anna—Mary's mother—at the moment of Mary's conception. About this mysterious force, Emmerich said:

> *This holy thing, concealed in the Ark of the Covenant in the fear of God, was known only to the holiest of the high priests and to a few prophets. . . . It was the work of no man's hands, it was a mystery, a most holy secret of the divine blessing on the coming of the Blessed Virgin full of grace.*[15]

As such, Emmerich envisioned the Ark of the Covenant becoming flesh for the first time in the conception of the mother of the Lord. While the Ark had symbolized for previous generations the containment of the covenant, Mary came to represent its next stage—an unassuming human vessel who not only contained the new covenant but issued it forth in the form of a divine person.

Through my research and daily spiritual practice, I have come to realize that Mary resides within each of us as a *pattern of complete responsiveness to Spirit* that can alone bring us into a co-creative relationship with the Divine. Becoming aware of this latent capacity is, no doubt, a necessary first step; but giving way to it may involve a protracted struggle with fears, feelings of unworthiness, or conflicting religious beliefs. Thus, between the awakening and the full acceptance, one may experience years of denial—and even forgetfulness.

The following stories all involve a childhood encounter with Mary that, for various reasons, the recipients set aside until later, when crisis or spiritual yearning caused them to reach into the past and find her—the ark of a new covenant within themselves—ready to be opened.

Four years ago, I had one of my final sessions with Rachel, a woman whose other visions of Mary are included herein.[16] She came into therapy originally to deal with the effects of being raped ten years earlier, and by the progressive erosion of her self-esteem from having been married to an alcoholic for twenty-seven years. Our work together proved to be intense and difficult, but she was eventually able to overcome her deep fear of expressing her needs in relationships. She was almost ready to leave therapy about a year before; but she elected to stay a while longer, attending a weekly therapeutic dream group and scheduling an occasional one-on-one session. As it turned out, recalling and reliving the earlier pain was not enough: Rachel also had to reclaim a vision of herself that had been lost to her. One event, which signaled the beginning of the end of our work together, was Rachel's recall of a memory that she had long forgotten—a memory of seeing Mary when Rachel was only sixteen.

The catalyst for Rachel's recollection was a lecture that I had given on modern-day encounters with Christ and Mary. Rachel wanted to attend but had been out of town. So she obtained the tapes of the morning-long presentation and played them in her car tape player. She admitted to me later that she had been somewhat critical of my interest in these traditional religious topics. And yet, as she drove down the road listening to the lecture, she was moved in spite of herself by a forgotten memory that came back to her after forty-one years. She pulled over by the side of the road and wept.

Rachel explained to me that when she was a child, her parents urged her to stay out of the swamp next to their property. But she was drawn to go there and decided, in this case, to ignore their wishes. One tree in particular called to her, so she often sneaked away to climb it. There she found the sense of freedom that eluded her in a family where she was often misunderstood. So Rachel escaped to the swamp and to her special tree—not so much to run away from home, but to find a home for herself.

One day she went into the swamp and climbed her tree. Peering through the woods to the other side of the swamp, she could see the new Catholic school that was almost finished. And there she could see, out in the courtyard, a statue that had not been there before. Wanting to get a closer look, Rachel climbed down, crept through the woods and walked out into the clearing where the new statue stood. It was made of cement, all grayish white; but it was adorned with wreaths of fresh roses. A ceremony must have just taken place, Rachel thought. The stone figure was of a girl about Rachel's age. Although Rachel had been raised a Southern Baptist, she knew that the girl was supposed to be Mary; and yet she was surprised by Mary's youthfulness. As she marveled at this, Rachel was startled to see the face of the statue gradually transform into the living face of a young girl. The girl had deep blue eyes, and beamed down at Rachel a most loving smile. Stunned, Rachel thought to herself, "You're like me!"

And then the girl said, *"Yes, Rachel, I'm just like you."*

Rachel never told anyone about the experience, and quickly forgot about it. Why would anyone forget such a momentous event? Since then, I have discovered in my work as a psychotherapist that this is commonplace. Indeed, I have found that we typically forget two types of extraordinary experiences: traumas that are too painful to bear, and uplifting experiences that exceed the upper limits of what we consider possible for ourselves. It is easy to understand why people suppress the memory of emotional and physical trauma. But too often, it seems, we also suppress the good news about ourselves that we simply cannot accept as true.

As Rachel told me of her recollection, tears of relief and gratitude ran freely. She admitted that she had rejected the gift from Mary. She had rejected Jesus, too, because Jesus was who her family worshipped; and she couldn't accept much of what they stood for. So as an adult Rachel rejected Jesus and Mary, and turned to the East and found a guru to follow. But after remembering her encounter with Mary, Rachel said that she realized that Jesus and Mary had always been there for her. "I am so happy," she said, "that I have found them again."

Carl Jung once said that the healing of the psyche inevitably involves a spiritual cure. Rachel's recollection of Mary's declaration of their essential sameness was the spiritual intervention that Rachel needed to begin her life anew: It helped to restore her sense of unsullied goodness that had been lost for half a lifetime.

Since the modern Marian apparitions began 150 years ago, the principal witnesses of Mary's presence have been children. We know of their encounters because they went public with their experiences—either because they wanted to, or because their friends and family refused to keep the experiences confidential. But in spite of the many stories that have been told, others have never been revealed. Indeed, at least some young visionaries have managed to keep their encounters from public scrutiny—either by remaining silent as Rachel did, or by telling people who, in most cases, simply dismissed the stories as childish fabrications.

It might seem that the encounters that have been kept secret— and then often forgotten—amount to a wasted resource that could have served the needs of others, as well. If the purpose of every encounter with Mary—and other spiritual beings, for that matter— is to communicate to the masses through the visionary, then this assessment makes perfect sense. But if the purpose of the Marian encounter is, first and foremost, to establish and cement a relationship with God through the Blessed Mother, then the dissemination of messages can be seen as merely one way that this relationship might bear fruit in the visionary's life.

Even though the recipients of these quiet, isolated encounters with Mary often forget about them until much later, the experiences seem to represent a kind of early spiritual conception that germinates slowly in the dim recesses of unconscious memory. It makes sense that the vision breaks through early in life because most of us are more open to such experiences then. The Divine enters through the portals of childhood innocence, sinks into forgetfulness, and then resurfaces later in the midst of a crisis to redirect and deepen the course of the person's life.

So many mystics have reported that the awareness of the Divine breaks through when we are least likely to expect it—when we are quietly musing, thinking of those we love, or expressing our joy over simple things. The German mystic Jacob Boehme (1575–1624) experienced his first spiritual illumination as he contemplated the beauty of sunlight reflecting off of a burnished pewter dish.[17] Similarly, in the following account a little girl is surprised as she celebrates the beauty of springtime, and her devotion to Mary, in her backyard.

> *It was in the early 1950s and I was between the ages of six and eight. Our family lived in a small central Texas farm town where the majority were Catholic, and I was enrolled in the local parochial elementary school.*
>
> *One day my father gave me a wooden apple crate he had gotten from the local grocer. I was delighted with the crate and placed it on a small table in our backyard. There I decided to build a shrine or grotto to Mary. Each afternoon after school I joyously "played" by creating my shrine.*

Turning the "shrine" or crate on its side, I placed inside an old plastic statue of Mary—about eight inches in height that was white and had features painted in black. Each day I searched for old containers that would serve as vases surrounding the statue, such as jar lids and cans. While today it seems all this could have been accomplished in mere minutes, I remember it taking me days. It was my mission to search each day to find just the "right" items, and I recall discarding things I deemed unsuitable. At last, all seemed ready one day. I gathered a few flowers from my mother's gardens and even some small wild flowers, added water to my "vases," and placed this in the shrine around and about the statue. Then I began singing some songs to Mary, and about Mary, that I had learned in school. I recall even dancing to the songs—which I had not learned in school.

While I danced, I glanced at the shrine and became transfixed. The statue had taken on colors! I dropped into a sitting position and continued staring at the shrine. The face had real skin tones as did the hands; her dress was white, but now a crystalline white, and her mantle on her head was blue—quite soft in color. She held a crystal rosary that reflected soft rainbowlike colors. She was "real" and very humanlike. She looked very calm, serene, and peaceful. And although she first looked down toward her bare feet, she lifted her eyes slowly without moving her head and smiled sweetly at me. There were no words, but I knew without being told that she liked the shrine.

I don't know how long we gazed at one another, but I then received a strong compulsion to get pencil and paper. I dashed into the house and retrieved them, and returned to sit cross-legged in front of the shrine. I drew the Lady as

I saw her. She remained perfectly still as I did so. I could only draw stick figures, yet I drew her likeness as easily as if I were an artist. I was using a pencil on a scrap piece of paper, but the picture appeared colored—flesh tones, white, blue—in exactly the same hues as she appeared. The drawing of her was about 2½" to 3" tall. She, by the way, was appearing about the same size as the shrine statue with cloudlike gauze or a film around her. It never occurred to me during this entire time that this was odd or strange. I felt no fear nor questioned any of it. After I finished the drawing, we looked at one another for a while and then she "melted" away. I was left staring at the plastic statue. I looked at the drawing and I saw it in colors.

Days passed—I continued to "play" at the shrine although not every day as before. I never saw her again, but strangely I felt no urge to want to—as if one visit was sufficient. I had hidden the picture and told no one about it or the "visit." This was not from fear, nor lack of sharing. I simply never thought about telling anyone—as if it was a highly personal thing. Many months later winter came, and in our preparation for it my family and I cleaned out the backyard. I put the weather-beaten crate in the trash/burn pile along with the dear flowers, jars, and lids. I stuck the statue in a drawer where we kept broken religious items. I showed my parents the drawing one day, and did not mention the colors I still saw in it. I was quite put out when they said, "Oh, you traced a picture of the Immaculate Mary. Go color it." It was then that I saw it in pencil and not in colors.

I kept the drawing for many years tucked away; yet, whenever I looked at it, it was a sketch done in pencil. I even

*began to doubt, as I grew up, that I had drawn it. One day I
threw it out.*

*My life has proceeded on a crooked route, and at one point
I turned my back on my religion. Surprisingly though, I always
kept a rosary by my bedside even if I did not pray it. Four years
ago something happened in my life that turned me back to my
God. Before seeking him, however, I turned to devotion to
Mary—who I feel led me back to him. That is when I recalled
vividly my Lady's visit from youth. As I write it now, I can see
mentally the entire scene as clearly as I view this pen and paper.
It is a scene of utmost peace, serenity, and simple beauty.* (S.O.)

S.O.'s experience never made the headlines. It never impressed
her priest or her congregation, nor produced documented healings
in those around her. And yet, her encounter differs from
Bernadette's initial vision at Lourdes in only two insignificant ways:
It occurred only once and no one else found out about it. In other
more important ways, it bears a great deal of similarity: The young
woman in her vision never spoke and she remained unidentified,
and yet a profound relationship was established in the course of the
brief encounter. As we shall find, this silent, ambiguous introduction is by no means unusual. Something of great significance is
conveyed without a single word. Like the historic Mary who left us
her life—not the written word—as a testament for us to contemplate, these encounters offer a silent invitation to join her in serving
God. If, as an ancient meditation text says, "all methods take their
source in quietness,"[18] then Mary exemplifies in these subtle
encounters what may be the pinnacle of spiritual practice—that is,
the dynamic stillness of mind and openness of heart through which
the Divine can reveal itself in all of its splendor.

Those familiar with the series of apparitions at Lourdes will detect a similarity of *feeling* between Bernadette's first encounter and S.O.'s experience. Bernadette exhibits a shy but openhearted wonder as the apparition acknowledges her without a word. According to Bernadette's own story, she heard a loud rustling in the hedge above the grotto called Massabeille. She saw the hedge moving, and then saw something white in the shape of a young girl. Bernadette stared at the girl for a moment and then knelt to pray the rosary. The girl showed Bernadette that she, too, had a rosary on her arm, and then walked into the grotto, disappearing from view.

In this first meeting, the two parties are not, as yet, fully acquainted: The relationship points to the indeterminate future. Even so, it is hard to imagine the relationship proceeding without this quiet experience of shared mutual regard and common spiritual practice. Indeed, Bernadette's introduction to the girl may have seemed relatively rushed and impersonal without this period of quiet mutual contemplation.

Whenever more than one person experiences the presence of Mary, the likelihood that the experience will become publicized greatly increases. When Lucia and her cousins, Francisco and Jacinta, witnessed their first apparition of an angel at Fatima, Lucia urged the other two not to tell anyone. Lucia had learned to be discreet the hard way: When she went for her first confession, she emerged from the confessional to find several people laughing at her for what she had said. Fearing that people would again ridicule her, Lucia hoped that she and her cousins could keep their experience between them. But Jacinta eventually broke the silence, and Lucia proved to be right about the ordeal that ensued.

In the following apparition of Mary, two sisters encounter her together. But unlike the Fatima seers, these children succeeded in keeping their vision a secret.

When I was about ten and my sister eight, we had a vision of the Blessed Mother.

It was a beautiful summer day. They sky was blue—no clouds. It was very quiet—no other people, animals, cars—nothing.

Then we looked in the sky and there she was. She was in dark clothes. She had dark hair.

We knelt and prayed. We walked home, agreeing not to talk about it or to tell anyone.

About five years ago my sister and I were at a dinner. My sister and I sat across from each other.

She said, "Do you remember, when we saw the Blessed Mother near Nannie's (Grandmother) house?"

I started nodding my head and I said, "Yes, I remember."

After that dinner, my sister and I were able to recall and share with others that experience of long ago. (J.A.)

Like so many of the visions in these chapters, J.A.'s apparition resembles an abbreviated form of one of the major historic apparitions. Among others, J.A.'s experience brings to mind the apparition at Pontmain, France, in 1871. It was there that Mary appeared in the evening sky above a snow-covered landscape to a farmer's son, Eugene Barbadette, aged twelve, who had gone outside into the barnyard to see what the weather was like. Eugene's brother, Joseph, who was ten, soon joined him, and was able to see the apparition, as well. Above them they saw a smiling woman dressed in a deep blue star-spangled robe, wearing a golden crown. Over the course of the next three hours, many people gathered in the barnyard as the boys reported what they saw and the changes that took place in the apparition. Three other children from the town joined the gathering later and were immediately able to see the

Lady, as well. However, none of the adults—including two nuns and the local priest—could see anything except three "stars" that remained visible only for the duration of the apparition.

During the three-hour barnyard vigil, the children observed letters appearing on a broad streamer that lay at the Lady's feet. The children slowly spelled out three messages: *"But pray my children," "God will soon answer you,"* and *"My son allows himself to be moved."* Toward the end of her manifestation, she held a red crucifix upon which Jesus was hung. Her grief was profoundly evident, but her original state of joy returned again just before she disappeared from the night sky.

At that time, the whole region was under the threat of takeover. Napoleon III had declared war on Prussia in July of 1871, and thirty-eight of Pontmain's five hundred inhabitants were immediately conscripted. Within weeks, the French had suffered terrible defeats; and by January, the Germans had advanced to a point only miles away from Pontmain. A takeover of the area seemed imminent. The apparition appeared on the eve of a sudden reversal: The soldiers withdrew within days, and peace was declared.

Some people believe that Mary manifested to urge the people to intervene with their prayers in a situation that could still go either way. If so, the prayers of a few people figured heavily in the outcome of the war. Regardless of whether the group's prayers served to turn the tide, Mary's celestial appearance coincided with an unexpected turning point in what seemed to be a hopeless situation.

The purpose of the Pontmain apparition seems clear on the surface: to awaken hope and faithfulness in a despairing people, and to urge them to make a difference through their prayers. But the particular details of the Pontmain apparition remain universally relevant. Indeed, the lack of specificity in the Pontmain message actually increased the applicability of the vision in the context of later times and places. Even though a general message might frustrate our desire for more specific responses to our particular needs, it withstands the passage of time more easily than a message that concerns only immediate problems. The more *general* the message, the more it transcends the original context that gives rise to it.

And so, we can see that Mary's characteristic silence in these initial encounters enhances the meaningfulness and widens the applicability of the experience. Like Jesus, who often frustrated his audience by his silence and brief enigmatic responses, Mary says a lot by saying a little, and thus ensures the relevance of her manifestations for years to come.

We have seen how Mary manifests to individuals early in life as if to implant an idea that only later flowers into its full expression. Understandably, this initial manifestation can provoke a variety of responses. In the accounts we have examined thus far in this chapter, the children have welcomed Mary's presence. But if the purpose of Mary's manifestation is to prepare a person for a later spiritual awakening, the response of the recipient at the time of the original vision probably does not matter very much. Apparently, *whenever* the person acknowledges her, Mary comes forth at that time as a potent memory to affirm the presence of God in the person's life.

The following account supports the notion that a person's initial response does not prevent the vision from exerting a positive impact at a later point. Initially, the recipient may be frightened by the vision, but eventually the recipient may reclaim the experience years later when its value becomes more apparent.

I was five years old and lived in Grove City, Pennsylvania. My grandparents were going to take me to Florida for a vacation. We spent the night in Pittsburgh so they could visit some other relatives. The room I slept in was on the third floor, a converted attic to the front of the house. When I woke up in the morning the room was filled with white light. I just lay there looking at it when I heard a voice that said, "Turn around and look at the window." *Although I had never heard such a voice before, it didn't scare me, but I also didn't turn around. The voice repeated the statement a second time, and then the third time before I turned to look at the window. Then, three floors up on the front window was the most beautiful woman I have ever seen. She was wearing blue and white—a long veil and gown. She never said anything, just smiled the most beautiful smile.*

I had just been fitted for glasses and I can remember thinking she wasn't real, so first I rubbed my eyes and she was still there. Then I picked up my glasses and put them on and she was still there. Of course, I didn't need the glasses. She was just as perfect a vision without them as with them.

She was still there when I ran hysterical and crying for my grandparents to take me home. I wanted to go home. I never told anyone about the experience until I was an adult.

I never forgot the experience, but I did put it on the back burner through my youth. I was in my thirties when I started really questioning why it happened. Since then, I've turned into a serious seeker, always trying to do better and be closer to God. I've still not figured out the vision yet. However, it's likely that the experience was supposed to stick in my mind to nudge me on to the spiritual path.

One thing I've often thought about is that in all the different pictures I've seen of the Blessed Virgin Mary, none have captured her beauty, and none have captured her light.
(M.F.)

In M.F.'s encounter with Mary, she witnesses her indescribable beauty. This corresponds with virtually every reported "sighting" of Mary to date. Invariably, the witnesses say that she is exceedingly beautiful. Two seers of well-documented apparitions—Vicka from Medjugorje and Gianna Talone from Scottsdale, Arizona—have thought to ask her why she was so beautiful. In both cases, they heard her say, *"Because I love."*[19]

As we approach death, the barriers separating us from spiritual realities apparently dissolve. People who recover from life-threatening illnesses or injuries often attribute their healings to the luminous beings who appear to them as they hover between this life and, presumably, the next. But the healing may not originate from outside of ourselves: It may spring from the hope and faith released in encountering these loving presences who have been there all along. As these beings lovingly mirror to us our true natures, they may awaken in us our languishing capacity for healing and rejuvenation. Take, for instance, the following encounter with Mary.

I was about eight years old and my mother had kept me home from school because I wasn't feeling well. I had slept most of the morning and was running a fever which was steadily rising.

Just before noon, I remember getting up to use the bathroom as I had diarrhea. I don't remember much else until my mom came into the room to check on me. I recall her exclaiming, "What in the world!" and then she came and laid her cool hand on my forehead to assess my fever. Apparently I had become so delirious with fever that I had used the bathtub instead of the toilet to do my business. Mom knew this was getting serious. She cleaned me up and put me back into bed. My temperature had gone up to 104 degrees+.

We lived in a suburb on the outskirts of Minneapolis. The doctors were a forty-five-minute drive away, and Dad was at work with the only vehicle our family owned.

Mom tried to soothe me and get me as comfortable as possible. She left my side to call Dad to come home to get me and take me to the doctors as quickly as possible. While she was gone telephoning Dad, I had the most beautiful experience.

Beside my bed, the Virgin Mary appeared. She just stood there about two feet off the floor and smiled at me—the most beautiful smile that penetrated every cell in my body. Her skin was milky white; her eyebrows were very thin and arched and she wore a light blue cloth draped over her head. The cloth either had a white lining on the inside or she had a second white cloth draped beneath the blue one atop her head. Her garment was a robelike style of light blue and white. Everything about her seemed to be emanating peace, complete trust, and love. As she smiled at me, it was as though she spoke to me telepathically. I remember hearing her say, "Everything is going to be all right." *Then I closed my eyes and dozed off, feeling totally at peace.*

As luck would have it, Dad was out to lunch when Mom called so she left a message for him to call home as soon as he returned. I remember telling Mom, "It's okay. Dad doesn't have to come home. The Virgin Mary was here beside my bed and she smiled the most beautiful smile and told me everything would be all right. She was so beautiful, Mom!" *I said.*

Mom at first thought I was still delirious and went to get the thermometer to take my temperature again. I told her I was sure it would be back to normal . . . and sure enough it was.

Some people, I realize, would argue that diarrhea will often help reduce a fever, and I agree that that may have helped. But I know what I saw and felt. It is still as vivid today as it was over forty years ago, and I am very thankful for having been given such a beautiful memory.

I am also thankful for a very loving mother who has always been very open-minded, and has loved so unconditionally. (L.D.)

We can never know if Mary manifested to heal L.D. directly, or "merely" to mobilize L.D.'s own capacity to restore her health. If we see Mary or any spiritual being—as an external agent of healing, then we see ourselves, in contrast, as passive recipients in the process. From this perspective, Mary resembles a traditional physician, who restores us to health by introducing the necessary medicinal agent to destroy or offset the intrusive, debilitating illness. If, however, we see the vision as a spiritual catalyst who awakens our own inner dormant healing processes, then we in turn assume a more active role as we *respond* to the awakening power of her presence.

The greeting that Mary extends to a child can assume many forms but in virtually every case she affirms her love for the person—then and always. In the account that follows, the child leaves with a potent message that has reverberated throughout her life and ever since.

I've had many incidents in my life and the most special ones happened when I was attending St. Elizabeth's grade school in Wilmington, Delaware. I had two concerning Mary, and I'd like to tell them to you.

It was another heavy homework assignment, but this time I had to write two poems on top of all my other homework. One poem was to be for four or five stanzas long and the other three to four lines. Mine was a dysfunctional family, and I couldn't start my homework until my father went to sleep. I was still struggling with the poem while the clock ticked away. It was after 10 P.M. and I was tired and in tears. I asked God to please help me. I told him I couldn't go to bed until I had my poems because I was afraid to face Sister Julia if I didn't have my homework assignment completed.

The next few minutes I started writing and it sounded beautiful. I asked God for a title, and I wrote out "The Ivory Tower." Happy now that I was finished, I started to pack my books away when I remembered I still needed the three- or four-line poem. Almost falling asleep I prayed again, and this poem I remember.

> *All the flowers are in bloom,*
> *If more come there's plenty of room,*
> *But the one that is the fairest of all*
> *Is the Blessed Mother.*

As I put the poems in my binder, I remember thinking the writing was not like my writing: My writing was rounded and bigger, while these letters were smaller and looked different.

The next day we took turns, one at a time, putting our poems on Sister Julia's desk and returning to our seats. Sister Julia looked straight at me and ordered me to her desk immediately. I was puzzled by the redness of her face, which happened when she was angry. She pushed the poem at me and said she didn't want me to copy the poems from a book.

I quietly told her that I didn't copy them; I wrote them myself. This caused her to lose control. She accused me of lying and said it was possible that the short poem was mine, but since I lied about the other one that I was probably lying about that one also. She was furious that I also would let someone else write them for me. I told her that I had written them. That was the last thing I said because she ripped them in pieces and threw them in the wastebasket, and I had my knuckles rapped after which she ordered me back to my seat and she left the classroom slamming the door after her. I heard the whispers of the other children, but I could only look down at my desk. I wanted so badly to retrieve the pieces from the wastebasket, but I was afraid that she would enter the room and reprimand me again. I have thought over the years about being hypnotized to try to remember that poem, but I have so many terrible memories in my childhood that I have always been hesitant to pursue that.

The other incident with Mary happened in first or second grade. My classmates were putting their names into a box to see whose name would be picked to be Mary in our May procession. Well, I asked God and the Blessed Mother to please make sure that my name was not picked. I was ashamed of my old clothes and my hair, which was poker straight. Then right before they picked a name I heard a woman's gentle voice say, "I choose you." This was upsetting to me, and I hoped that I just thought I heard it. They picked a name and it was mine.

They were very special events that took place in my childhood, but it was many, many years before I realized just how special they were. (J.C.)

J.C.'s second experience with Mary resembles the experience of a woman who saw Christ appear to her at a prayer meeting. Moved to tears by the honor of seeing him, she asked mentally, "Why me?"only to hear him say, "*Why* not *you*?" Obviously his words conveyed much more to her than a simple answer to her question: With his question, he challenged her to disqualify herself in the light of his vast and timeless acceptance of her. Similarly, Mary's simple statement about choosing J.C. obviously goes beyond the context of her involvement in the May procession: Mary declared J.C. acceptable in that moment—and for all time.

At the beginning of our lives—before we have embarked on any conscious search for meaning—Mary exists within us as a potential to become a handmaiden to the process of the Divine working through our lives. As such, the Mary within us is easy to overlook. Her power derives from being in relationship with God and carrying the divine seed to fruition. Until we recognize the importance of fully entering a co-creative relationship as she did, our own responsiveness may shrink in insignificance alongside the qualities more often valued by the world.

Mary's manifestation in a childhood vision or dream provides recipients with a foretaste of their own latent capacity to serve God as she did. As a living Ark, Mary models for all of us the release of the virginal potential that remains so often dormant until we desperately need it. In the midst of adult crises, we might find her waiting for us in our dreams—if not also in the distant memories of childhood.

THE MIRACULOUS
Medal

C ATHERINE LABOURE, A NOVICE NUN IN THE convent of the Sisters of Charity in Paris, served as a transitional figure in the development of the modern apparition. As a cloistered nun, she was protected from the public scrutiny that was to plague later visionaries. Indeed, people only learned her name years later. She was older at twenty-three than most of the later apparition visionaries; and she was better off than many have believed, having become the mistress of a large farm at the age of twelve.[20]

In July 1830, Catherine was awakened in the middle of the night by a child dressed in white standing at the foot of her bed—a being Catherine later identified as her guardian angel. He beckoned for her to follow him. She rose from her bed and followed him down the hall into the chapel of the convent. On her way there, she was amazed to find candles lighting her way down the hallway. As she entered the chapel, she encountered Mary for the first time. She heard a sound like the "rustle of silk," and then saw Mary enter the room and sit in the father director's chair. Catherine fell on her knees and knelt before Mary, experiencing the "sweetest moment of her life." Meanwhile, Mary spoke to Catherine about the tragedies that would befall France in the years to follow, and of a mission that she wished to entrust with Catherine. When Catherine looked up later, the child was still there, but Mary had disappeared.

Later that year, Catherine saw Mary again, this time while meditating with the other novices in the chapel. Catherine again heard a sound like the rustle of silk, and looked up to see Mary standing beside a picture of Joseph. She was surrounded by light, and gem-colored beams of light shown from her fingers as if to represent her gifts to the world. Mary slowly turned in an oval frame, and the reverse side showed itself to Catherine. On this side was the letter *M*, a cross, and two hearts—one encircled with thorns and the other pierced by a sword—and the words, "O Holy Mary, pray for those who have recourse to thee."

During another vision two months later, Catherine saw the entire scene again. But this time, Mary told Catherine to have this image struck as a medal that people could wear. After a canonical inquiry, permission was granted in 1832 to have the medal produced. At that time, an epidemic of cholera gripped Paris. When the medal was distributed, those who wore it exhibited a remarkable immunity from the disease. Today, millions of Miraculous Medals have been produced, and countless miracles credited to it.

2

A LOVE BEYOND
Words

"Then many times she remained silent;
we were silent and she was silent. . . .
She said she was looking at her children."
Conchita of Garabandal, Spain

WE HAVE OBSERVED THAT WHEN MARY MANIFESTS
to children for the first time, she often says very little or remains
silent altogether. Even so, her silence in the initial meeting does
nothing to mute a profound sense of presence that the recipients
feel then and later, even though years of forgetfulness may lie in
between. In the accounts that follow, the reader will again observe
that when Mary manifests to adult visionaries, she often says little to
them, as well. We might ask, Why would Mary remain silent during
an encounter that the recipient may never experience again? Surely,
it makes sense that she would take advantage of the fleeting moment

to leave the recipient with something specific that might positively influence life choices from thereafter.

Although a verbal exchange between ourselves and Mary might seem more desirable and more advanced than a silent encounter, it is by no means clear that such an exchange is better. Indeed, her silence may represent the most effective form of communicating to those of us who might latch onto words and miss the bigger picture. Perhaps the appearance of Mary accomplishes all that is needed to stimulate and deepen one's relationship with God. In support of this view, we would do well to consider another famous apparition in which not a single word was spoken—the apparition at Knock, Ireland, in 1879.

The Irish had suffered for more than thirty years from recurrent devastating potato blights, which had left the population of Ireland decimated. Out of desperation, tens of thousands had immigrated to America on crowded, unsanitary ships. Many died in transit. The soul of the nation had been shaken by this protracted tragedy.

In 1879, the final year of the potato blight, Mary appeared to a group of people in the village of Knock. On a windy, rainy August evening, the local archdeacon's housekeeper, Mary McLoughlin, set out to visit some friends. As she passed the outside of the beautiful church, she saw what she believed at first to be three statues. She thought that Archdeacon Cavanaugh had ordered them, and had left them outside until a suitable place could be found for them. With other things in mind, she went on past and visited for a while with her friends.

Later, when she headed home by the same route, Mary was startled by the sight of the luminous figures even from a distance of several hundred yards. As she approached and examined the scene more closely, she could see that the figures were not statues at all, but ethereal images floating about two feet above the ground. The Virgin Mary, clothed in a white robe and wearing something resembling a crown, stood in the center of the scene with her arms stretched out in front of her and with her eyes turned heavenward as though in prayer. She was flanked by two men that people later decided had been Joseph and the apostle John. To one side could be seen a simple altar upon which a lamb stood, facing Mary.

Mary McLoughlin ran off to call others to see what was happening. Before the figures disappeared about two hours later, fourteen people had visited the supernatural scene. A fifteenth witness viewed the scene from half a mile away, and could only see a "large globe of golden light." Unlike other major apparitions before and since, neither Mary nor the other figures spoke a word; and no one reported receiving any interior messages, or "locutions." Further, the figures were incorporeal: When one woman tried to kiss Mary's feet, her lips were greeted by only the wet brick wall of the church.

Ironically, when the housekeeper went about notifying people of the miracle, she urged Archdeacon Cavanaugh to go out and see the miracle; but he misunderstood her and thought that the apparition had already ended. Widely known for his charisma and his profound devotion to Mary, Cavanaugh may have been the human catalyst of the apparition. He said afterward, "I have regretted ever since that I omitted to do so. God may will that the testimony to his Blessed Mother's presence should come from the simply faithful and not through his priests." [21]

During the apparition at Knock, Mary remained entirely silent and unmoving while fourteen people weathered the wind and rain to marvel at the luminous figures of Mary, John, and Joseph floating just above the ground. Yet, the absence of a verbal message did not deter the populace from attributing the greatest significance to the event: Our Lady of Knock became immensely important to the Irish people, and has been credited with numerous miraculous healings. The church, as well, accepted the apparition as authentic. Despite her silence, Mary's presence worked its way into the imaginations of those who saw her or learned about her appearance afterward. Like a painting that permits the beholder to arrive at his or her own interpretation, the apparition at Knock left the Irish people free to discern Mary's message for themselves in the context of their own personal and collective concerns. No matter how far removed we are from that time and circumstance, her silence still frees us to do likewise, even though a century has since passed.

The encounters in this chapter resemble the apparition at Knock in one significant way: Mary remains silent throughout. While many of us would gladly exchange the ambiguity of her silence for the guidance that her specific words might bring to us, her presence wordlessly communicates a profound meaning to the visionary—a meaning perhaps more subtle and complex than words could ever express. In the final analysis, it may be true that words are often a poor substitute for what silence alone can convey.

Indeed, we will observe in the following encounters that Mary's quiet presence accomplishes several things at once: It allows for a communication that is beyond the capacity of language to convey adequately; it models the state of quiet receptivity that we may need to emulate if we hope to become channels of the living Spirit; it evokes an awareness of those things that may stand in the way of a continuing relationship with her; and, finally, it serves as an invitation to a relationship that may, as yet, require more preparation on our part.

Silence is the Highest Language of Love

The deepest exchanges between people typically occur in silence. Experience informs us that words too easily trivialize the complexity and richness of love in its deepest forms. We often stop talking and become very still when we feel profound love for someone. Or, we may talk about other things, choosing to preserve the sanctity of the relationship by avoiding mention of what matters to us the most. And so, sometimes silence is about a love so deep and so accepting that it goes without saying.

To illustrate the power of silence to communicate an almost overwhelming love and sense of peace, let us consider the following waking vision of Mary.

About twelve years ago, I went to my first healing Mass led by Father Kellerher. I got there at 7 P.M. The church was already crowded, and I took a seat over on the right-hand side. I knew that Father Kellerher would appear at 8 P.M. Meanwhile, we were being led in the rosary and in charismatic singing.

As I prayed, suddenly I had a vision of Mary. She was standing about seven rows up on the right-hand side, just above the pew. The bottom of her feet were about three inches from the top of the end of the pew. She was dark skinned with very thick eyelashes. Her dress was blue, and she wore a long outer jacket that had gold stars on it, all of which were shimmering. The jacket also had a gold border all around it. Her hands were joined as if in prayer, and there were golden stars around her head and shoulder area. She kept her eyes almost entirely closed. The peace that she emanated was lovely. I don't know how long she stayed. As I breathed in her essence,

I felt overwhelmed. Then I heard a rustle and Father Kellerher came out. He walked over to the very spot where she manifested, and she disappeared as Father began talking. He would go sideways or a little forward, but he always returned to the spot where Mary stood, as though he was being drawn there. I could feel that she loved him. (T.P.)

In her vision, T.P. witnessed an image of Mary similar to what the children saw in the sky above Pontmain, France, in 1879—a woman dressed in dark blue with gold stars adorning her garments and surrounding her head. T.P. has had two other waking encounters with Mary, and two with Jesus. In every instance, they remained totally silent as they manifested to her; and yet, in every case T.P. understood the reasons for their appearances without having to be told. Apparently, much can transpire between the seer and the seen in the virtually unlimited medium of silence.

Silence May be Mary's Principal Message

In addition to providing a powerful medium through which the deepest love and blessings can be bestowed, Mary's silence may also represent her central message to the recipient—that is, *to be still and become a vessel of the living Spirit.* From this standpoint, her nonverbal presence intimates our own capacity to attain that state of expectant stillness in which the Divine might find its greatest pleasure. As a model for us, her silence subtly challenges us to nurture a quiet yearning that remains entirely pliable to Spirit.

I have encountered this lesson in many of my most memorable dreams, including a recent dream about Mary herself.

I dreamed I was looking at a statue of Mary. I was studying the statue's face closely when, to my surprise, it began to come to life!

Her head moved and she smiled at me a most joyous smile. I let out a cry of surprised delight, and the statue promptly resumed its lifeless appearance. But then, as I sat quietly again, her face moved and she smiled down at me, as if to say, *"If you will remain still, I will come to life in you."*

This dream brought to mind other dreams from my past that, while differing somewhat in content, conveyed the same essential message about the importance of quietly allowing the Spirit to have its way with us.

In one, I was outside in a nighttime setting. I looked up and saw an orb of brilliant white light approaching. Knowing that I was dreaming and that I was seeing the eternal Light, I cried out in anticipation, only to see the Light retreat, as if awaiting a quiet, more receptive response. I bowed my head and turned my eyes away from it. Then the Light came down upon me, awakening a painfully intense sense of love and ecstasy.

In another, I dreamed I was lying awake in my bed and the Light came again. As it coursed through my body, I gave myself to it as much as I could. The energy grew more intense and the light more brilliant. I realized in that moment that when the Spirit comes to us, *we must remain entirely quiet and receptive* if it is ever to consummate its purpose within us and through us. It is what Mary did when she accepted her role in the advent of the new covenant, and it is perhaps what she invites all of us to do now.

In the following dream, Mary comes to the dreamer—literally out of the clear blue—in the midst of a power outage. M.J.'s encounter with Mary comes to her only after everything familiar has failed her.

I dreamed that I was at the office standing in the doorway, and someone came up behind me and said, "The computers have all quit working!" I looked at the computers, and just as I did they quit working and the lights went out. I looked around and saw that the entire suite of offices was dark. It was so still and quiet; not a sound could be heard. "A storm must be coming," I thought.

The office is at a corner and there is a window on each corner wall. From the doorway, I looked toward both windows but could not see anything. I walked over to the window on the right. I looked up at the sky (we were on the sixth floor of a seven-story building). The sky was a beautiful blue with a couple small fluffy clouds. Then I walked over to the window on my left. I looked up at the sky and saw again that it was a stunning blue. Just then a big fluffy cloud moved into sight. It was hovering just above the seventh floor. I thought, "That cloud is really low and beautiful." As I was looking at it intently, it opened up and Mary, the mother of Jesus, appeared as if in a picture. But then as I looked closer I could see she was not a picture. I thought, "Is that a statue of her?" Just then she moved and looked right down at me, right into my eyes. I was so startled to realize she was alive that I jumped back into the room about two feet back from the window. At the same time she moved from the cloud into the office window. We were face-to-face and I was speechless. I was awestruck, as well, by the intense sensitivity and compassion in her eyes. Love emanated from her. I understood that she was projecting her love to me without her having to say it.

I then began to move, as if gliding, backward away from her. I wanted to stay with her: I knew she wanted to say something more to me. I started to cry and pleaded with God not to make me wake up, but God told me that I had to wake up now but that there would be more later. (M.J.)

The collapse of the usual hubbub of activity leaves M.J. open to encountering Mary in what is perhaps the only climate conducive to her coming—complete silence. In this dream, we can see how the Divine enters our lives through the quiet openings created by the unexpected.

As M.J. stands face-to-face with Mary, she knows that Mary loves her *without having to hear the words.* She feels this deeply, and lacks for nothing in that precious moment of profound mutual regard. She wants one thing—for the experience never to end. But when it does end, she finds that she can bear the anguish of separation; for she knows that a relationship has been established and that they will be together again. This promise of a future reunion is, perhaps, the only thing we have to cushion the pain of separation from such presence. This yearning—activated or intensified by such encounters—keeps us in a state of anticipation; and it keeps us forever wondering if what we do and what we think takes us closer, or farther away, from the promised reunion. It gives our life new meaning and intensity, even though we might never be quite as contented as before.

Like M.J., most of us never find God through our own directed efforts. We have to be caught unawares during emotional and spiritual "power outages"—when unexpected changes or setbacks leave us quietly open to surprises. This is one of the paradoxes of the spiritual path: The search itself gets in the way of the openness we need to allow the Spirit to enter our lives. Consequently, we may ultimately have to abandon the search and be taken by surprise.

To illustrate, my friend Walter Starcke, who is a modern Christian mystic and author, is fond of telling about his first break-through experience in meditation. He was concentrating intensely and doing all the right things, but was getting nowhere. He felt that it was hopeless, so he finally gave up trying. As soon as he did, the holy Light burst upon him for the first time; and he was over-whelmed by its power and love. Consequently, he thought that he had found the secret! It was in letting go, he realized. So the next day, he proceeded to repeat the process, but to no avail. Finally, he decided that it just wasn't going to work, and the Light came again! He realized later that there is simply no way to orchestrate letting go, and that the moment of illumination always comes as a surprise—and often on the heels of a genuine sense of failure.

The following meditation encounter with Mary closely resembles M.J.'s dream.

Mary came to me while I was meditating. Her face appeared right in front of me, and she looked at me without speaking. I felt that there was no separation between us, and I felt a great sense of quietness and humility, knowing that my true nature was as her own, that is, spiritual.

I remember especially the colors. Her eyes were clear blue, like the drape around her head and body—a beautiful sky blue. Her hair was yellow like the glow I saw around her head. She held out a pink rose to me, which I understood to be her gift of love. I could smell its sweet fragrance.

But then, I began to doubt what I was seeing, and thought that I was perhaps making it all up. At that point, she began to fade from view.

When I let my judgmental mind go quiet again, she returned in full brilliant color—blue, yellow, and pink. (M.W.)

In this vision, M.W. experiences Mary approaching her and bringing an intense, almost overwhelming sense of love and presence. But, like my friend Walter, M.W. discovers that Mary's coming depends on her remaining open and suspending the intrusive analysis and judgment of her mind. M.W.'s encounter also resembles my own experience, recounted above, in which the statue of Mary came to life only so long as I could suspend my excitability. M.W. faced a similar challenge, that is, to hold in abeyance the intrusive doubt that so easily shatters our moments of deepest intimacy. To this end, Jesus said that we must become as "little children" to enter the kingdom.

> *"Truly I tell you, unless you change and become like children, you will never enter the kingdom of heaven"* (Matthew 18:3).

In M.W.'s experience, one can observe that the whole experience hinges on a singularly open state of mind that for most of us remains elusive—if not entirely buried in our memories of a more innocent time.

Silence is a Powerful Intervention

When a person who is important to us remains silent without explanation, all kinds of feelings may stir to life—such as curiosity, self-doubt, and intensified yearning. We may spend a lot of time trying to interpret the silence, and we will inevitably learn more about ourselves than about the other person in the process.

It is easy for us to overlook the evocative power of intentional silence in relationships. Talk is everything in our culture, and silence typically connotes indecision, passivity, or downright dislike. As a psychotherapist, however, I know that one of the most generous things I can do is to remain silent and noncommittal at important junctures in my work with my clients. Silence may not be what they want from me, but it causes them to consider *how they are seen* from a more objective viewpoint, and *what they might do for themselves* in the absence of external feedback and assistance. Of course, they may imagine many true and untrue things about me—that I judge them, that I do not care for them, or that I am bored. But whatever a person experiences in this ambiguous context will usually reveal the work that they still need to do on themselves. Indeed, silence from those who matter to us stirs feelings and memories that otherwise remain untouched by the surface talk of day-to-day human contact. In the midst of the experience of intentional silence, one learns whether fear or trust, passivity or initiative, will fill in the spaces created by the ones we care for the most. Without saying a word, the presence of a silent witness can awaken us to the presence of unfinished business or neglected duties that may have prevented further spiritual development. And out of all of this can come a life-reorganizing question, What do *I* need to do *now?*

From this standpoint, Mary's silence can be seen as a form of intervention. By silently revealing herself to us, she creates an opening in which we may discover what lies, as yet, between ourselves and a more complete relationship with Spirit.

Silence Prepares us for a Deeper Relationship

Building on the above idea, Mary's silence may indicate that the recipient is in the early stages of a relationship that can eventually sustain a fuller exchange with her—when and if additional growth takes place. Mary's silence may, therefore, testify to the recipient's unreadiness, while mobilizing the recipient to do whatever is necessary to enjoy a more complete exchange.

Some of the most famous Marian apparitions evidence this process of silent preparation and gradual deepening. Bernadette encountered Mary several times at Lourdes before Mary spoke to her; thereafter, a period of instruction ensued, whereby Bernadette received personal guidance as well as information that was intended for others, as well. The seers at Garabandal, Spain, witnessed the coming of a silent angel on several occasions before Mary appeared for the first time. Similarly, the seers at Fatima, Portugal, experienced the presence of an angel on three occasions before Mary herself appeared to them. The angel, who identified himself as the angel of peace, guided them to pray unceasingly, and gave them communion on the occasion of his final visit. In each case, these initial visitations served as a clear preparation for a more complete relationship with Mary. The implied message throughout was, *You must be prepared for a relationship with me.*

Thus we can see that initial encounters with angels—or silent visitations from Mary herself—introduce the visionaries to, and prepare them for, a relationship that may eventually graduate into an ongoing exchange between Mary and the seers.

I have stated previously that I believe Mary manifests in our lives to activate a potential within ourselves similar to the "greatness" that was hers as the mother of the Lord, and that her silence in these encounters conveys the spirit of openness and surrender required for such an undertaking. She comes to awaken in us our capacity to *contain* the Spirit, to *carry its promise to term,* and eventually to *give it a life of its own* through service and love.

Conveying this silent message, Mary appeared to another woman as a plump, all-loving motherly presence.

Earlier this year I was in prayer, and an incredibly intense beam of light came to me. My eyes were shut. I know that

Light. *For me, it is Christ. It is very laserlike, and cuts clearly and sharply, and has a message for me when it comes. Usually I focus on the Light and attune myself to its message, which I did on that particular night. But this time my eyes shifted, and behind the Light I saw Mary in her own light. Her light was very soft, almost orange in color. She was on the plump side, and very, very motherly. I felt so much love— so much unconditional "I love you just as you are" kind of love. She had her arms wrapped around her plump body, as if her body was the entire cosmos.* I knew her love was for absolutely all of creation. *I knew that I was surrounded by those loving arms and was completely in her care and protection.*

Looking back, I think the intense, male light of Christ was being balanced by the round, full, gently feminine love of Mary. It was as if I was seeing two levels of consciousness manifested side by side. They were different, but each was a part of the greater whole. (A.T.)

As she gazes upon a silent Mary, A.T. understands something that eludes the descriptive power of language. She apprehends a way of being that assures her of Mary's love for her and all of creation, and provides subtle encouragement to embrace life in the same fashion. So much is communicated in that moment, and nothing of importance is left open to question. A.T. knows that Mary loves her and loves all of creation. She knows that this warm, loving presence stands behind and quietly supports the discriminating and expressive power of the Christ Spirit. And she knows, as well, that what Mary did, she can also do.

From our above consideration of Mary's manifestations, we can see that her silence does not limit the importance of the meaning of an encounter with her. To the contrary, it accomplishes several important things at once. It allows us to receive her love in an undiminished and unburdened form. It intimates our own "virginal" capacity for receiving the Spirit in a state of expectant stillness. It catalyzes an unassisted review of our life and of our readiness for a relationship with her. And it invites us to do the things necessary for a more complete relationship with her and the Christ Spirit.

Silence may also be Mary's distinctive way of bringing our relationship with her—as an externalized tangible presence—to a close. At Lourdes, for instance, Bernadette encountered a silent Mary at the beginning *and* at the end of her appearances. Pelletier suggests that Mary's silence in these initial and final encounters at Lourdes was a particularly meaningful aspect of these apparitions. He believes that her silence underscored the importance of two aspects of Catholic religious observance—the rosary and the scapular. About Bernadette's final vision, he says:

> *It was a silent but obvious preaching of the scapular, just as her teaching of the rosary had been silent but eloquent. . . . This silent message was like a last testament, something she kept until the very end because she wanted to impress us with its importance. . . . Her last visit . . . was an invitation to wear the scapular as a symbol of placing ourselves under her protection.*[22]

By remaining silent, Mary directed Bernadette's attention to how she could continuously experience Mary's presence even after she had gone—in particular, through the use of the rosary and the wearing of the scapular. Beyond the uniquely Catholic connotation of these two symbols, the rosary signifies for all of us the *practice* of Mary's principal teaching—that is, to pray unceasingly. And the scapular, which represents a piece of Mary's mantle, bestows upon its wearer the continual *presence* of her motherly protection.

Both of these religious symbols—when embraced as ongoing practices and attitudes—give us the means *to do the work* and *to awaken to the presence* of the Divine through our own self-directed efforts. They thus serve as sufficient substitutes for the externalized presence of the Divine, freeing us from the dependency upon such phenomena. This is, perhaps, as it should be; for ultimately, we are bound to discover that any external demonstration or message—no matter how dramatic and evidential—leaves us wanting more. In our search for something ultimately fulfilling, we may even come to doubt the authenticity of what once inspired and moved us. Ultimately, we will probably discover that anything that is only "out there" cannot feed the soul for long.

If Mary spoke eloquently to our every need, then we might never engage in the spiritual practice that we need to do, nor awaken to the subtle motherly presence that can embrace us from within. In time—like the visionaries who have seen Mary appear for a season and then leave them—we discover that the true measure of her presence becomes not so much what we can see or hear, but how fully her spirit lives within us. As our spiritual practice matures, and our internalization of Mary's essence progresses, she apparently recedes from view, quietly beckoning us to find her within ourselves through spiritual practice and a constant invocation of her motherly embrace.

La Salette

IN 1846, THE MODERN ERA OF APPARITIONS BEGAN:
A beautiful woman appeared in a cloud of white light to two
children, aged fourteen and eleven, in a meadow near the alpine
village of La Salette, France. The two unlikely seers—Melanie
Calvat and her fellow cowherd, Maximim Giraud—described a
single experience of encountering a woman who emerged out of a
cloud of white light, and sat on a rock to speak with them tearfully
about God's displeasure toward the region's inhabitants, and about
coming crop failures.

Since the two children hardly knew each other, and lived some
distance apart from each other, people found their identical story
credible and soon concluded that the woman had been Mary. The
church authorities, however, spent a great deal of time and effort eval-
uating the apparition, and interrogated the children on numerous
occasions before declaring it an authentic manifestation of Mary.

Melanie and Maximim of La Salette were the first visionaries to
receive secrets from Mary. At first, people did not realize that the
seers were keeping information back. But the children admitted,
under subsequent questioning, that the beautiful woman had also
given each of them messages that they were told not to reveal. When
she spoke privately to each child, the other child was unable to

overhear the conversation. So, neither child was able to confirm or deny what the woman shared with the other.

For months, everyone assumed that this information had been personal in nature. Without the children's input, however, some people seized upon the idea that Mary had given them prophetic information. As this belief took hold, the children still refused to comment. Unprotected by religious vows or convent walls, the two simple children quickly found themselves caught between two worlds. They wished to remain loyal to the woman who was clothed in light; and they wished to satisfy the church and the public's needs for information. But they could not do both. In the context of their silence and the public's unbridled speculation, their "secrets" eventually became the focus of intense controversy. Withholding this information put the young seers at odds with every priest and parishioner who wished to know more. In the face of all of this, the children valiantly protected the secrets through grueling interrogations.

Whatever Mary originally communicated to the children at La Salette, we can be assured that the apparition experience became a "malleable product" shaped by the intense pressures placed on the seers from the public and the church. Not surprisingly, the La Salette seers eventually succumbed to pressure, recorded their secrets, and sent them in sealed envelopes to Pope Pius IX. But by then, the "secrets" may have been altered by the seers due to external pressures and the passage of time. Melanie, in particular, was accused of embellishing the "authentic secret" with popular ideas that occurred to her before she finally wrote down her full account. While she emphatically denied the charge, many people who believed in the authenticity of the La Salette apparition were relieved when church authorities declared that the mission of the seers had ended.

3

MARY'S TANGIBLE
Gifts

"This is my precious gift that I leave to you."
Mary's words to St. Dominic
upon giving him the rosary

SOME TIME AGO, AFTER I HAD JUST BEGUN researching Marian encounters, I was taking a break from my studies and sitting on the sofa. I closed my eyes for a moment to think, and suddenly I lost track of where I was. For a few moments, I found myself in a place I had never been before—a Catholic church where apparitions of Mary were known to manifest. A priest spoke to me about the places in the church where Mary often appeared.

Then he said, *"To worship Mary is to worship the unmanifest."*

As I emerged from the trancelike experience, I found the priest's words puzzling, for they seemed to contradict the traditional view of Mary as the bringer of healing and other tangible gifts. But then as I pondered his words more deeply, I realized that Mary represents our capacity to carry and issue forth the very best of what we yearn for but which remains, as yet, unborn—that is, the Christ within. But while she points to the unmanifest, Mary also responds in very concrete, practical ways that can provide a foundation for one's faith.

I am reminded of the story[23] of a king who asked a spiritual teacher to teach him how to meditate. Knowing that the king loved his collection of precious jewels above all else, he told the king to meditate on his jewels. Rather than resisting the king's desires, the teacher knew that the beauty of gems could serve as the best means to focus the king's attention and to inspire a deep yearning for God. As the king followed the teacher's surprising advice, he received spiritual illumination and went on to become a famous teacher in his own right. In so many of the great stories of spiritual awakening, we learn that the path to God is through, not around, those things we yearn for the most.

We know that from the beginning of Christianity, people have petitioned Mary's assistance in resolving every human problem great and small. And, as countless testimonials indicate, such petitions often succeed in manifesting tangible results. For instance, the following woman experienced what was clearly a miraculous healing as a child, apparently through Mary's intervention.

Kathy was born with a congenital condition that rendered one of her arms totally useless. Apparently the nerves that normally control the arm muscles were simply nonexistent. The doctors at Johns Hopkins even recommended amputation since the limb would remain forever unusable. Indeed, Kathy's brother was born with the same condition; and to this day, he cannot use his arm at all.

Despite the doctors' assessment, Kathy's grandfather turned to Mary for help. As the little girl slept in the bassinet, he placed a small statue of Mary at one end of her little bed. He was not much of a believer, but he loved his granddaughter. If he had been the king in the story, then Kathy would have been his jewel; and he was willing to do anything to preserve the beauty he saw in her. The next morning, Kathy woke up and began moving her previously limp arm! When the doctors examined her later, they found the limb normal—which they declared to be impossible. To this day, she is normal in every way.

The mind may resist the obvious; but history tells us that calling upon Mary makes one's prayers especially efficacious, and their results particularly concrete. For instance, Nancy Fowler, a visionary who has witnessed a series of monthly apparitions at her farm in Conyers, Georgia, relates the story of how Mary assisted her in finding just the right car for herself.[24] It might seem odd that the Blessed Mother would get involved in that level of mundane detail, but it seems that the more we open ourselves to her, the more she participates in every dimension of our lives, helping to bring into our experience whatever good that has been previously lacking, or unmanifest.

Many of us pray for the right partner, having had too many mismatches in our lives. When one woman prayed to Mary for assistance in meeting the right man, Mary appeared to her—but then so did Christ, as though the petition reached him through the Blessed Mother.

On Mother's Day, I went to church and was kneeling before the Blessed Mother. I told her that I was so tired of meeting the wrong men, and that I wished to meet the right man for me. While I was praying and crying, Christ appeared beside me. He was dressed all in white. He put his arms around me and said, "Everything is going to be all right now, everything is going to be all right."

I went home knowing that the right man was coming.
(C.W.)

C.W. had no doubt that Christ's words would come true in a literal way. While there is no way of knowing whether Christ's words referred to an eventual relationship, C.W. elected to interpret them that way. She did everything she could to prepare for the meeting that she was convinced would soon happen. It didn't happen instantly. Actually, she met her future husband at a wedding some time later. But throughout, C.W.'s faith never waned. She said, "Once or twice since then I've said to myself, 'Did this really happen?' But he was there with me. I believe he was physically in the room with me."

In my own practice as a psychotherapist, I often pray for the Blessed Mother's assistance in my work. The first time I ventured into this form of "therapeutic" petition was about seven years ago.

I had been working with Barbara weekly, if not more often, *for eleven years*—which still stands as a record for me—and still she needed medication and regular psychotherapy. Tragically, she had remained almost totally resistant to medical treatments for her lifelong clinical depression. She had been treated unsuccessfully by a foremost expert on depression in this country. She had taken every antidepressant medication available, without obtaining any lasting relief. She had then undergone electroconvulsive therapy, which had a negative effect on her; then she tried to kill herself. Then she came to me when I was fresh out of graduate school.

Daunted by the challenge that she represented, I tried many therapeutic roles and interventions before finally just settling into a caring, supportive role with her. That is when she began to get better, for no one, she said, had done the incredibly simple thing of just listening to her. Thereafter, we worked well together; and she made modest progress as we explored the story of a tragic past that included rape, betrayal, and parental desertion. She was always willing to share her dreams, no matter how hopeless she felt. Her dreams clearly suggested that she would someday recover, but I did not know how or when it would happen.

I often prayed for Barbara; for there were many occasions when I felt deeply concerned about her state of mind, fearing that she would try again to kill herself. Then, one day while Barbara was in my office, I silently asked Mary to intervene. It felt especially appropriate, for Barbara had lacked nurturance all her life. I never told Barbara, who was a Baptist by upbringing, that I asked Mary to intercede on her behalf. Anyway, within a couple of weeks, Barbara returned to my office looking and sounding better than ever before. Neither of us could account for the improvement. She terminated her counseling soon after, and—as far as I know—has remained free of the crippling mental illness that had burdened her since an early age.

The most famous instances of Mary's manifestations suggest that her love becomes especially concrete as we petition her for help. Legend has it that Mary handed St. Dominic the first rosary during a time in the early 1200s when he was working diligently to convert the Albigenses in southern France. Mary gave him something to hold on to—not merely some idea or a message—that would organize and anchor his spiritual practice, as well as provide a practical method of praying that he could teach to others. In other encounters, she introduced scapulars and religious medals whose concreteness give their wearers a sense of reassuring closeness to her and Christ. It is easy to dismiss such artifacts as unnecessarily primitive, but the Blessed Mother has become known for bringing about measurable changes that give our faith a foundation that we can see and touch.

Even today, Mary's impact is often felt in very tangible ways. Well-known Marian phenomena include spontaneous physical and emotional healings, the fragrance of roses, a silvery sun spinning in the sky, colored lights around religious shrines, rosaries that turn to gold, and weeping statues. Further, these signs of her presence frequently manifest without an attendant visual apparition: People feel Mary behind the phenomena even though they may never see her.

In the following accounts, the recipients experience many of the ways that Mary has been known to manifest her love in tangible ways. They emerge from their experiences having been given something tangible to indicate, without doubt, that they have been blessed by her loving presence.

G.W.'s miraculous experience came as an answer to her need for help. Suffering from a paralyzing fear of driving an unreliable car, she received a surprising blessing.

When a dear friend decided to move to Florida, she gave me a twelve-inch statue of Mary flanked by two kneeling angels and encased in a heavy metal frame. It was one of two statues given to her by her deceased mother.

I placed the gift on my carpeted bedroom floor—upright against the wall and under my sewing machine cabinet— until I could find the perfect place to hang it. As busy as I was at the time, the gift remained there for longer than I had intended.

In the meantime, my automobile was giving me a bit of

trouble. It seemed to hesitate whenever I turned a corner. I complained to my husband, and he exchanged cars with me for a couple of days but did not experience the same problem.

We exchanged cars once again, and the hesitation was still evident to me. That night as we were preparing to go to bed, I confessed that the car was making me very nervous, and that I was afraid it would die on me as I turned onto a major highway. He assured me that it would not do that; and since he was a service manager and former mechanic at a Cadillac dealership, I could take his word as being reliable. I finally fell asleep, still worrying despite my husband's assurances.

I don't know what woke me in the middle of the night, but I raised myself up and turned around. I had been sleeping on my right side with my back to the bedroom door. I was amazed to see a beautiful golden light surrounding our floor-length mirror that was situated in the corner near the door and next to my sewing machine cabinet. The light then slowly expanded to cover the entire corner. It was, without a doubt, the most beautiful sight I had ever seen. I was so awestruck that I failed to wake my husband. When I finally thought to do so, the light had disappeared.

When the alarm woke us the following morning, I told my husband of my experience and he agreed that it could not have been a light from outside since our blinds were tightly closed to keep any light from disturbing our sleep. Therefore, it had to have had a supernatural source. But I wondered, What was the light's message?

The answer came as I was standing in front of my dresser mirror combing my hair later that morning. Something told me to turn and look at the frame under my sewing cabinet. There, situated between Mother Mary and the angel on her left side, was a small object that had not been there previously. I walked over to the frame and removed the object. It was an old worn medal from the Sacred Heart Auto League, blessed to protect the owner while driving his or her automobile. Needless to say, I went into a state of euphoria. This was a gift from Mother Mary to ease my troubled mind and heart. I felt that I need not worry any further about driving my car.

Still, I felt the need to phone my friend in Florida to be certain that the medal had not been placed there by her mother. She assured me that her mother had not put it there, and that she had never belonged to the auto league. Further, she insisted that no one in her family had ever owned such a medal. She also told me that she had thoroughly dusted the frame and statues before giving it to me. I was then convinced that it was a gift from the Virgin Mother, and that the golden light was the aura of her presence in our bedroom.
(G.W.)

While the mind may balk at the idea that Mary would, or even could, materialize a worn Sacred Heart Auto League medal, such stories have the power to convince us that such things do happen. Even so, we might ask, Are such physical assurances desirable? Won't they lead to a childish dependence on tangible proofs of God's love? Indeed, it often seems more spiritually mature to disregard such primitive demonstrations of God's love.

Certainly, we should not base our faith exclusively, or even primarily, on tangible symbols, gifts, or intermediaries of any kind. And yet, faith can be activated—and, perhaps, sustained—by observable symbols and inexplicable phenomena that temporarily arrest the mind's tendency to undermine everything that it cannot see or measure. For G.W., the auto league medal in her pocket was obviously not the treasure itself; it only pointed to the loving being who cared enough to allay her fears during a frightening time. But its comforting physicality will doubtless serve as an important pointer again and again to that which truly matters to her.

Mary's most recognized "calling card" has to be the fragrance of roses. In the following account, F.L. experiences this tangible gift while meditating in a group. For her, it marked the beginning of Mary's influence in her life.

At the age of forty, and as a mother of two, I entered the depths of a marital transition and personal crisis. So I began to try various "therapies" to help myself. Not much worked until I began to go deep inside and listen to my heart instead of my mind. Gradually, as I surrendered to God and allowed the light of Jesus to fill me up, I felt the presence of the Divine Mother.

In the summer of 1994, I attended a meditation and healing group where the healing presence of the heavenly Mother first came to me. At first, I did not know for sure if it was just my imagination. But while meditating with a group of women, I began to feel very relaxed and open. At this point, I began to smell a very strong fragrance of roses. I remember thinking, "Boy, Melissa sprayed a lot of air freshener around. This is unbelievable!" Then I began to feel extremely warm from the inside out. Eventually, the outside of my body became very warm, but not uncomfortable. It seemed as though there was a glowing presence all around me.

As we ended our meditation, we went around the room to talk about what we had experienced. I discovered to my surprise that no one smelled the roses—except my friend Barbara, who was sitting right next to me. She told us that she, too, smelled the distinct fragrance of roses. Then, as I shared my experience, I noticed how wet I was. You could actually see moist droplets on my skin; however, the glowing warm feeling was no longer there.

About two weeks later, I visited a woman who does spiritual counseling. She only knew my name—nothing else. She began to meditate and pray for me. About halfway into the meditation, she stopped in the middle of a sentence and said she felt the presence of the Virgin Mary with me; and this had only happened with her a couple of times before.

At this point she started sweating and said she felt very warm, just as I had during the group meeting. After that session I felt pretty convinced something special had happened to me.

Then, about a month later, I was talking to a lovely old woman about her life. At one point, she said, "Excuse me a minute," and went into the other room and got something for me. She said, "Here, I'd like you to have this. It's for you." I had told her nothing about my Marian experiences. I opened this small envelope she gave me and saw a beautiful silver picture of Mary with the Christ child in her arms and accompanied by two angels above her. I almost started to cry, and I asked her why she had given this to me. She said, "I don't know, but it's yours now." I carry the medal with me always, and look at it from time to time and thank Mary for being in my life now and always. (F.L.)

Unlike G.W.'s experience with the auto league medal, which happened all at once, F.L. experienced Mary's growing influence as a series of related events. Nonetheless, her three experiences culminated in a similar way—with the gift of a physical reminder of Mary's love. Again we see how our connection with Mary is symbolized and anchored by objects that we can hold, even as we may yearn for what we cannot see or touch.

Those who pray the rosary often report a tremendous protective and healing force associated with their devotional practice. For example, there is a well-documented story of four Jesuit fathers who were stationed in Hiroshima during the Second World War. They had just finished their morning Mass at the very moment that the first A-bomb exploded and killed half a million people. Father Schiffer, one of the surviving Jesuits, described what happened to him just as he prepared to eat his breakfast.

Suddenly, a terrific explosion filled the air with one bursting thunderstroke. An invisible force lifted me from the chair, hurled me through the air, shook me, battered me, whirled me 'round and 'round like a leaf in a gust of autumn wind.[25]

He was apparently knocked unconscious, because the next thing he remembered, he was lying on the ground, opening his eyes. He got up and looked around, and saw that every other building in the area had been leveled to the ground. His only injury was a few pieces of glass in the back of his neck. Even though the American doctors assured the men that they would become ill from the radiation, none of them suffered any effects. Father Schiffer attributes their miraculous survival to their devotion to the Blessed Mother, and to the regular practice of praying the rosary.

From such dramatic accounts, we can see that prayers to Mary can bring dramatic measurable changes in people's lives. Like many others whose accounts are included herein, E.M. did not turn to Mary until she was desperate. As a nonpracticing Catholic at the time of her crisis, she reached into her religious heritage and found the rosary. And through the rosary, she rediscovered Mary, who apparently catalyzed both a financial reversal and a spiritual reawakening for her.

On April 19, 1991, I received a layoff notice from a high-tech firm where I had been employed just over a year. Two years earlier, I had received a layoff notice from a similar firm, where I had been employed for over seven years. The first experience had been very traumatic, but this second lay-off absolutely paralyzed me. I did not know what to do next, since the high-tech industry in the northeast was in chaos, and almost all companies in the area were downsizing their work force.

The following Thursday, I went to a spiritual study group that I had joined a year before. For some reason, the Medjugorje experience of one of our members came up for discussion just before people began to leave.

John had visited Medjugorje the year before; and, in filming the sky at six o'clock in the morning, he captured on film cloud formations that looked like the Blessed Virgin and the head of Jesus wearing a crown of thorns. After his experience, John gave me several things about the Marian apparitions to read and to share with others.

This new information came at a time when I had already begun to turn to Mary. At that time, my anxiety level *was extremely high due to my increasing financial burdens. I carried a large mortgage on my home, a $400-a-month equity loan, and an equally high car payment. All of this, and I had only been given a month's severance pay. It was a horrible time. So I began doing novenas[26] on a daily basis. When the fear escalated to the level of panic, I would turn to the rosary to calm myself down. I was also petitioning Mary for her help.*

While I welcomed John's material, it was several days before I finally sat down to read it. As I settled onto my couch on a Tuesday afternoon around two o'clock, I felt a sudden stillness in the room. A stream of sunlight shone through the front windows, and I had a fleeting thought of perhaps adding sheers to keep the sun from fading the carpet. Slowly, but noticeably, the light coming through the window changed from yellow sunlight to a soft golden tone. The light also changed from slanting in from the window to a straight up-and-down shaft. I sensed rather than saw that someone else was in the room. I looked around the room to see whether or not it was my dog, but he wasn't there. I looked back at the light and it was still straight up and down, as though someone was standing there.

Then, I hear a voice in my head gently say, "Don't worry, everything will be all right."

I knew at once that it was the Blessed Virgin Mary. "Why can't I see you?" I asked silently.

"Because you already believe," *she said. And the brief experience was over.*

The light changed again, back to yellow sunlight and slanting in from the window. I sat mesmerized for over an hour.

Four weeks later, I was hired at a higher salary than I had ever earned before. The firm was also in financial trouble and I knew that the job would not last, but it paid the mortgage and other bills until I could sell the house.

For myself, the experience lifted my self-esteem which was in the wastebasket by that time. I had always found it easy to get jobs before, and the experience of losing two jobs was one I had never dreamed of facing. Before the Marian experience, I felt worthless. After the experience, I felt that if Mary took the time to come to tell me that my life was going to be all right, I had importance "up there."

Not only did my experience make me feel better, but it was a spiritual awakening for me. I went back to the Catholic church, but I still felt something missing. The only pleasure I seemed to get from life was reading and discussing with other people ways in which we might get closer to God.

Since my encounter, Mary has not let me down. I have been supported financially even though I've had to use my savings sometimes. I am still in the process of transitioning from my old life to a new one, but I'm happier than I've ever been in my life. I attribute my transformation to the Marian experience. That she took the time to reassure me still overwhelms me with gratitude. (E.M.)

Many of us shy away from praying for specific positive changes in our lives. It seems too much like telling God what to do. "Thy will be done," we utter, asking God to direct the course of our lives. But in trying so hard to avoid telling God what to do, we may never consider what we want in the first place. In *Alice in Wonderland,* for instance, Alice encounters the godlike Cheshire

Cat sitting in the tree at a fork in the road. She asks the Cat for directions.

> *"Would you tell me please which way I ought to go from here?"*
>
> *"That depends a good deal on where you want to get to."*
>
> *"I don't much care where," said Alice.*
>
> *"Then it doesn't matter which way you go," said the Cat.* [27]

Jesus said, "I will do whatever you ask in my name" (John 14:13). He never said that we had to be vague about it. In teaching us how to pray, he did after all say, "Give us each day our daily bread," not, "Nourish me if it suits you." I think that stories such as E.M.'s career reversal appeal to us because they remind us that our desires, when combined with our willingness to submit to higher will, give the Divine a place to start working in our lives. Without expressing a clear wish—however trivial it may seem—the forces of healing and transformation may remain idle in our lives.

Of course, personal crises force us out of hiding to reveal what it is we want. Like E.M., we suddenly decide that saving a life, a job, or a child's arm is worth petitioning the Divine without concern for the relative merits of our requests. Through such passionate prayers, we expose our vulnerabilities, and by doing so we finally enter a relationship where we become fully revealed—which may be the point at which the Divine can, in turn, become more fully revealed to us. In regard to this idea, Lewis says:

> *By unveiling, by confessing our sins, by "making known" our requests, we assume the high rank of persons before Him. And He, descending, becomes a person to us.* [28]

In the following account, L.H. experiences an evolving relationship with Mary through her willingness to "unveil" her desires and to ask Mary for assistance with various practical matters.

Prayer has always been an important part of my life. However, most of my prayer time has been spent praying for others, and not very much for myself.

Then, last year my father and I began looking for some property in upstate New York. We had actually been looking for some time, and yet we possessed very limited funds. Consequently, we became very discouraged when we saw what we could afford. In July, my father announced that he was ready to give up hope and stop looking, but I begged him to continue looking with me. Without my father's help and partnership, I knew would never realize my dream of owning my own property.

That night in a cry of desperation, I turned to a prayer that I hadn't used very often; but it has always been one of my favorites—the Memorare (see end of chapter). It is a prayer that invokes the Blessed Mother Mary to intercede on someone's behalf and grant their petitions. I prayed to her and meditated for help in our quest for this property. Having faith that if one should ask to receive one should also make an offering, I promised our Lady I would make a shrine to her and my Lord Jesus if she would only help me in my quest. I also told her that I would be indebted to her for such a great blessing.

At that very moment I was never more sincere in my prayer. Exactly three days later I received a phone call from the broker, and he told me about a property. From the phone call description it didn't sound like what we were looking for and the price seemed too good to be true. Most properties in that range were far from our needs. The broker insisted that we should see it, and I told him I would get back to him. I called my dad, and he said maybe we should check it out.

That night I had my first encounter with divine intervention. The previous days had been busy, and I had almost forgotten about my request to our Lady. Nevertheless, in a series of dreams it was revealed to me that this was the place for us. In one very intense, very vivid, almost lifelike dream, I saw the most beautiful face of a woman whom I believed to be the Blessed Mother. Though I don't remember the words she spoke, I will never forget the impressions she put upon my mind. She revealed to me that this place was a very special place that was to be given to me, and that the shrine to her and Jesus should be located where others could see it. I knew she wanted it to be a special place for prayer and meditation.

Little did I know that this was only the beginning of my spiritual transformation at the age of thirty-three. The real estate closing went smoothly, and the first thing that I did was to set up the shrine.

During this time, I also set up some hunting blinds for the upcoming deer season. Another dream of mine was to hunt on my own land and to have a successful hunt. So it was on opening day at 9 A.M., I was given a four-point buck. Immediately after the take I raised my voice in thanks and prayer to God and to the spirit of the deer for his sacrifice for me. With the ease of the hunt I knew that I had been truly blessed.

With all the physical work and strains of my job, however, my body became wracked with pain by the end of the year. I went to the doctor; and he informed me that I had carpal tunnel syndrome in both wrists, a pinched nerve from a small fracture in the wrist to the elbow area, and patella softening of the knees, the latter of which was the most painful of my problems.

On New Year's Eve I didn't go out, since I could not even walk. I lay in bed tortured by pain in my legs. In desperation I prayed to Mother Mary and invoked her help once again, all the while thanking and reminding her of the help she had given to me before. Again, I promised her in return for help and healing I would do whatever she would ask of me. The next day was Sunday, and after Mass, I spoke with my spiritual director about the Marian apparitions. He asked me to follow him to the rectory where he gave me a rosary ring[29] and a scapular, and told me about the Legion of Mary, a group devoted to the work of the Blessed Mother and Our Lord Jesus Christ.

He explained that Legion members volunteer their services two hours a week, pray the rosary daily, and attend a weekly meeting. Well, right away I had doubts, and I told him my work schedule was very hectic and changeable. But that Sunday evening I had another very intense dream.

In it, Mary made it known to me that this was the work she wanted me to do. She told me not to worry about my job, and to tell them that I needed time off to attend the Legion meeting. She assured me that all would work out just fine and to put my faith in God.

The next day I told my boss that I was going through this "spiritual thing" and that I simply had to attend the meeting! I encountered surprising little resistance, and I went to the meeting. Since Our Lady asked for my service, I joined without further hesitation. Today I volunteer in hospitals and nursing homes where I visit the sick and elderly. I also assist at Mass and spread her message wherever I can—that through her we will be led to Jesus Christ.

Since I began all of this, my entire life has changed. And oftentimes little miracles happen to me. My body is free of pain and suffering, except for on occasion when I think it is to remind me of the blessings I have received from Our Lady and Lord. This new spirituality, this new path, has led me to helping and caring for the sick and less fortunate, and doing what I can to bring God's love into the world.
(L.H.)

L.H.'s overall story conveys a rich interdependency between herself, Mary, and nature to the point where hunting and ministering to the poor coexist harmoniously in L.H.'s deepening relationship with the Divine. As we follow her through her experiences with Mary, we see that her evolving relationship prepares her to serve others in a fuller way than ever before. The acquisition of the right property, the personal empowerment of successfully hunting on her own land, and the healing of her physical conditions obviously represented to L.H. desirable goals in their own right. But eventually it becomes clear that Mary's interventions were designed to serve a greater overall plan—to activate a greater capacity in L.H. to serve the needs of others.

When we are on the outside looking in—when our spiritual lives are impoverished by an excessive preoccupation with material ideals, fears, and personal gain—we may find the spiritual testimonies of others hard to accept. Our minds may resist believing, and our hearts may remain closed. But when we engage in daily devotion, our hearts and spiritual faculties gradually open up to the realities that are, apparently, always there for us. Not only can we accept the testimonies of others, but our own capacity for the miraculous expands until we, too, have a story to tell.

An Hispanic couple—both of whom are devout Catholics—told me about a remarkable apparition that their whole family experienced together in the summer of 2001. Again we can see that concerted prayers to Mary can bring about miraculous phenomena observable to others.

> *It was about nine or ten o'clock at night, and my wife, Mary, and I were sitting up in bed praying the rosary, as we do nearly every day. We were almost finished saying the final prayers, and I was deeply absorbed in the process. I opened my eyes briefly at one point and noticed something that was in the mirror facing the bed. I could see the image of the sacred heart of Jesus! It started off very faint, but then it got brighter, from the waist up. Jesus was mostly red, but his heart was white light.*
>
> *I leaned to one side and continued marveling at the vision. Finally, I told Mary what I was seeing. She opened her eyes and saw something, too. But instead of the Sacred Heart, she saw the Virgin of Guadalupe! I couldn't see anything but the Sacred Heart. But as I looked at it, it would come in and then go out. Then finally, as the image faded away, the image of the Virgin of Guadalupe came in its place, and I could see her, too. Mary could see both of them,*

as well. The images began to alternate, with one of them retreating to the rear as the other came forward.

Then we called our kids to come into the room. We didn't tell them what we saw because we wanted to see if they could perceive it without our help. We thought they'd be able to, since they pray the rosary with us. We just asked them if they saw anything in the mirror. They were able to see it, too, and described the same alternating images of Jesus and Mary! We finished praying the rosary together, and then we went to the kitchen. Later, we went back to look at the mirror again, and it was still there.

When we'd look at the apparition, we'd feel something, too. It wasn't just seeing something "out there" it was also an experience within. As we looked at it, we would feel something so good, so warm, and so sweet.

It was still there the next day, so we called my aunt to come over and to see if she could see it, too. We asked her the same question—if she saw anything in the mirror—but she didn't see anything. The vision gradually disappeared. (R.C.)

R.C. and his wife clearly regarded the vision as a gift of the highest order, but they did not consider it unusual. Living as they do in constant prayer, they have come to expect such things. There is a saying, "He who expects little will not be greatly disappointed." R.C. and his family know what can happen if we expect a lot.

As we have seen, Mary often manifests during times of worry and doubt to assure us of God's love and protection. In the following encounter with Mary, R.S. receives the assurance of Mary's protection during a time when she was worried about the well-being of her elderly mother. Again, we see how Mary consents to reach down to where we are, and to show us the caring that one might expect from one's own mother.

During my life (I am fifty years old), I have had a number of encounters from Jesus, most frequently during meditations and sometimes during special church services such as funerals. The most dramatic was a vision which I will share secondly. First, however, I wish to share my first and only encounter with Mary, which took place during the Christmas holidays of 1994.

I went home to Georgia to be with my children, mother, friends, and extended family members for Christmas. I stayed with my daughter who lives in the Atlanta area. My mother came from north Georgia to my daughter's house to be a part of the holiday festivities. After visiting several days, my mother prepared for her drive back to north Georgia. After exchanging hugs, "I love you's," and tears, I watched as my mom backed out of the driveway. I did what I have done a thousand times before: I said a prayer for her safe travel. Much to my surprise, a vision of Mary suddenly appeared standing on the hood of my mom's car. She was dressed in soft, flowing garments and a drapelike veil on her head which flowed down her shoulders and back. She wore a bodice of soft blue overlaid in white sheer drapes. The veil on her head was white.

Then I heard Mary say to me, "I will go with her."

My eyes instantly teared up; I was deeply touched. I responded mentally, "Thank you, Mary." I watched as my mom waved her final good-bye as she moved further away from the house. It was quite a sight watching the car move down the street with Mary standing on the hood of the car! When Mom arrived home she telephoned to let us know that she had arrived home safely. Her first words were, "I had the most pleasant drive home!" My mother has always been very special to me and my number one emotional support in my life. I am very thankful for her. (R.S.)

In virtually every instance of her intervention, we can see that Mary addresses an immediate problem while leaving the recipients to contemplate, as well, the larger implications of her presence in their lives. The words, *"I will go with her,"* not only reassured R.S. in that moment, but conveyed a promise reminiscent of Jesus' own words: "I am with you always, to the end of the age" (Matthew: 28:20). As such, Mary's surprising willingness to manifest the specific care and the comfort that we need during a crisis reveals a timeless promise that can, perhaps, sustain us in the absence of further proof.

In summary, Mary has long been associated with the materialization of miraculous phenomena, sacred relics, and healing and protection in times of need. Such miraculous, phenomenal manifestations are known as "prodigies" in the Catholic tradition, and seem to occur near the places where she has appeared. In Garabandal, for instance, Mary kissed innumerable objects submitted by the children—especially toward the end of her appearances—on behalf of the faithful onlookers. These personal items, in turn, became a perpetual secondary source of her blessings even after she ceased to appear. This dissemination of Mary's essence through kissed objects assisted the community of believers around Garabandal in sustaining itself somewhat independently of both the visionaries who, as we know, went through a period of doubt, and the local church hierarchy, which rejected the visionaries' claims. Indeed, the supernatural events and the blessed objects continued to inspire hope and faith in spite of Mary's eventual retreat and the controversy surrounding the apparitions.[30]

It had been six months since I had last seen Rachel—the woman who, as a sixteen-year-old girl, had witnessed a statue of Mary coming to life (see Chapter One). I found myself growing concerned; for even though she had terminated her counseling work with me, she had promised to write down her stirring childhood account of encountering Mary, and to submit it for inclusion in this book. Then, just before Christmas, I received a call from her in which she requested an appointment with me.

Three days later, she came into my office dressed in obviously new, stylish clothes. Good things had happened in her, and she radiated a joy that I had never seen coming from her before. She told me that she had come to thank me for my help and to tell me why she had waited to write down her story of encountering Mary.

She shared with me that after remembering the long-forgotten experience, she began to have her doubts. Why would Mary appear to her? Did the concrete statue in the school yard really come to life, or was it only her imagination? Who would believe her? she wondered. The more she thought about it, the more she discounted her own experience. It occurred to her that she had to know if it really happened; otherwise, she felt she could never share the story with others.

Around Thanksgiving, the opportunity arose to ask for some proof of her encounter with Mary. She had accompanied her husband to De Paul Hospital, a Catholic facility in Norfolk, Virginia, to have some tests done. While she was waiting, she decided to go into the hospital chapel. From previous experience of Catholic hospitals, she knew there would probably be a statue of Mary in the chapel. She crept across the hallway into the chapel and found herself alone there. A statue of Mary stood off to one side.

Rachel prayed for a while, then got up and walked up to the statue. She said, "I need to know if you really appeared to me. Please show me." As she looked closely at a statue of Mary for the first time in forty years, it suddenly moved. Once again, the face softened and came to life. Mary turned to Rachel and smiled.

As Rachel tearfully finished telling me about her recent encounter, she said that she still wondered how the statue could actually move and take on the appearance of life. Then she said that she knew from studying physics that matter is not the way that we see it at all, but is actually in a state of constant movement. She then speculated that there might be a way to alter its state and its appearance. Searching for something that might account for such a miracle, Rachel finally found the answer for her.

She said, "I believe love can do that."

Many of us would like to think that we are beyond the need for such concrete reassurances of God's love. But if we are honest, most of us retain a childlike fascination with miracles and a yearning for some kind of proof that we are not alone. Smelling invisible roses, seeing an apparition in the mirror, or observing a statue come to life, can give us just what we need to put our doubts aside and to open ourselves to the Divine in that moment and thereafter.

Surely, just as our relationship with our own mothers was forged in infancy through a nonverbal, tactile exchange, our highest spiritual aspirations still rest upon a foundation of early feelings that are awakened and sustained by concrete realities, and not by words alone. As we pass through the most difficult times in our lives, such objects and observable phenomena can serve as anchors in otherwise unstable circumstances. And as we hold to these things, our feelings can reach out beyond the forms to which we cling, and commune with the Being who brought to us these wondrous things.

Memorare

Remember, O Most Compassionate Virgin Mary,
that never was it known
that anyone who fled to your protection,
implored your assistance or sought your intercession
was left unaided.
Inspired with this confidence we fly unto you,
O Virgin of virgins, our Mother.
To you do we come, before you we kneel,
sinful and sorrowful.
O Mother of the Word Incarnate,
despise not our petitions,
but in your clemency hear and answer them.
Amen.

Lourdes

BERNADETTE SOUBIROUS'S ENCOUNTER IN 1858 with the apparition of a beautiful young woman at Lourdes, France, established a pattern that has been repeated in several instances since. It was the first time that the Blessed Mother appeared regularly over a period of time. It was also the first time that the public and the church had the opportunity to become involved in the process as it unfolded. It remains today one of the most revered and moving instances of Mary's manifestations, and has become the standard against which all subsequent Marian apparitions have been measured.

Bernadette's story is well known to Catholics and non-Catholics alike. Bernadette went gathering firewood on a cold, wet day with her sister and a friend. When the two other girls waded across a shallow stream, Bernadette stayed behind, apparently not wanting to get wet and cold due to her chronic asthmatic condition. Then she felt a gust of wind, and "something white" in the shape of a very beautiful girl appeared. Appearing to be around sixteen or seventeen years of age, the girl wore a white dress with a blue cape, carried a rosary on her arm, and had a yellow rose on each foot.

The girl remained silent during the first two encounters; but on the occasion of the third visitation, she asked Bernadette if she would like to meet her there every day for a fortnight. Bernadette said she would. Following the pattern set at La Salette, the girl revealed three secrets and made Bernadette promise not to disclose the secrets to anyone. Unlike many of the visionaries who were to follow her, Bernadette carried Mary's secrets to her grave.

During all of eighteen appearances of the woman, Bernadette never referred to the girl as Mary or the Blessed Virgin. She merely called her "Aqueró," a local dialect term that means "It" or "That one." At first, people were of the opinion that the girl was the ghost of a recently deceased local girl. It was only later that the public came to believe that the young woman was the Blessed Virgin.

At first, Bernadette was the only one who could see the woman when she appeared, thereby undermining her credibility with many of the onlookers and the local religious and civil authorities. However, two aspects of Bernadette's experience eventually ensured the ascendancy of Lourdes's to the status of an accepted apparition.

First, after Bernadette had pressed the girl to identify herself with no success, the girl finally revealed her identity in one of her last visitations: She assumed the well-known posture of Mary on the Miraculous Medal (that was given in a vision to Catherine Laboure), and said in the local dialect, *"I am the Immaculate Conception."*

Only four years before, Pius IX had declared the dogma of the Immaculate Conception, a widely held Catholic belief that Mary had been conceived without the stain of original sin. For young Bernadette to hear these *of all possible words* profoundly enhanced the status of her visions. Indeed, the local head pastor, who had remained skeptical up to that point, quickly reversed his stand on the previously controversial visions, and wrote to his superiors at once urging a formal inquiry.

Second, Aquero instructed Bernadette to ask the local priests to have a church built at the grotto, establishing what was to become a pattern of Mary advocating the construction of shrines and other tangible reminders of her presence. Coming from a mere fourteen-year-old girl, this message to build a new church greatly irritated the priests; however, the church authorities eventually complied with the request once the authenticity of the apparitions had been established.

Aquero also told Bernadette during the eighth of eighteen visions to dig with her hands into the muddy ground of the grotto. Complying with this strange request, Bernadette shocked the people around her by dropping to her hands and knees and digging in the mud. Many people promptly left the scene in disgust, concluding that Bernadette was surely deranged. But to everyone's surprise, Bernadette uncovered a previously underground spring, from which now flows 27,000 gallons of water every day. Just as the church obtained what it needed theologically, the public got something, as well—a concrete focal point for the abundant miracles that subsequently flowed from Bernadette's visions. By satisfying the disparate needs of the church and the public, Bernadette's visions at Lourdes became the most famous and accepted example of Mary's manifestation to the world.

4

THE HEARTBREAKING
Truth

"You will not be happy in this world, but in heaven."
Mary's words to Conchita of Garabandal, Spain

OF ALL HISTORIC RELIGIOUS FIGURES, MARY PROBABLY experienced the highest imaginable joy and the most profound, unimaginable grief. With God's blessing, she gave birth to a son who was the living expression of a new covenant between God and man. And then she saw her son misunderstood, degraded, tortured, and killed—while she remained entirely powerless to prevent it. Many have asked, Who suffered the most? Jesus? Or the mother who watched him die on the cross?

Given her exposure to the full gamut of human experience, it is understandable that Mary's appearances often parallel significant hardships in the lives of those who witness her presence. It makes sense that *if anyone can understand and comfort the suffering, she can.* In some cases, her manifestations come at the end of a period of difficulty and suffering; but in other cases, her presence foreshadows the onset of a lengthy struggle. The apparition at Pontmain in France came near the end of Germany's advance toward the village; and the apparition at Knock, Ireland, foreshadowed the end of the devastating potato blight. The apparition at Fatima did both: It promised the end of the First World War but prophesied the coming of the next. Mary's initial appearance at Medjugorje in 1981 did likewise. It served to bring healing to an area still smoldering from the racial atrocities of the Second World War, but it also preceded the renewal of racial unrest and civil war in the former Yugoslavia.

Regardless of when she appears, Mary typically manifests as an expression of grace and profound love in the midst of struggle—apparently to ameliorate the sense of meaninglessness and victimization that easily insinuates its way into our thinking. Further, her love empowers us to change what we can, and then to accept graciously life's inevitable hardships and losses. Mary's statement to Conchita of Garabandal, *"You will not be happy in this world, but in heaven,"* seems less a prediction of Conchita's personal unhappiness than a statement about what we all can expect, as well.

And yet, Mary's presence brings profound joy, as well. A compelling apocryphal tradition tells us that the resurrected Jesus went first of all to Mary to reveal himself to her before manifesting to his friends and followers. His adoring words, as found in Coptic apocryphal texts, underscore Mary' s gift to him and to the world:

> *Hail to thee who hast borne the life of the whole world. Hail my Mother, my saintly Ark. . . . The whole of paradise*

rejoices because of thee. I tell thee, my Mother, whoever loves
thee, loves life.[31]

If Jesus went first to Mary—and it is easy to imagine that he
would—then the woman who was the "first of the believers of the
new covenant," [32] and who presumably suffered the greatest loss of
all in the course of its unfoldment, also witnessed the first glorious
evidence of its fulfillment. When we examine what Mary means to
us beneath the surface of superficial associations, we are bound to
find that she is a most complex figure who brings joy and suffering
together within herself in a singular experience of love.

Many of us initially resist the idea that suffering is unavoidable.
We need not regard this as a weakness, for theologians and
laypeople alike find suffering to be the most difficult fact of life to
reconcile with a God who presumably loves us. How can he, we
ask, permit the suffering of innocent children, while at the same
time allowing cruel and malicious people to escape accountability?

Sometimes we know that our pain and suffering follow as a
consequence of our own unwise prior choices. Operating from this
perspective, we would like to think that we can avoid suffering by
paying off our debts, making amends, and living a virtuous life from
thereafter. But it takes a while before the effects from all of our past
actions catch up with us—and even if we could weather this process
with patience and dignity, we cannot reasonably hope to avoid new
mistakes and the consequent costs thereof.

Even if we *could* avoid all further error, a rational assessment
informs us that pain and suffering befall even those who lead
exemplary lives and deserve the best of everything. Sometimes the
capriciousness of nature inflicts suffering through natural disasters,
illnesses, and genetic deficiencies. And sometimes our suffering

comes, not from unwise choices or from nature's random thought-lessness, but from those who hate us without cause. In this case, we experience suffering when our goodness collides with those who are motivated by lesser ideals. Jesus' own plight at the hands of his contemporaries should tell us that we cannot reasonably hope to escape suffering by imitating him. But he knew that good could be better served by submitting to betrayal and death. Jesus saw beyond his immediate pain and *elected to suffer so that good could prevail.*

In meditating on the problem of suffering, I realize that there are two forms of suffering over which we have some degree of control. There is "payback" suffering that comes when we must account for unfortunate choices or mistakes that we have committed. We can learn from this suffering, but there is nothing particularly wonderful about the process. We can choose to accept this ordeal gracefully, or we can disavow any responsibility for it, preferring to complain about life's unfairness.

Beyond this process of endless accountability, there is "redemptive" suffering that comes from doing what is loving and right in a world where the loving thing is not always the safe or popular thing to do. If Jesus' suffering was payback, it was presumably for our sakes rather than his own; for nothing about his life warranted the suffering that he endured. As we contemplate Jesus' passion[33] and enter into his suffering vicariously, we experience *along with him* a less common form of suffering that comes from a willingness to put love above life itself.

Something strange happens when we identify with Jesus through his ordeal: We feel renewed and deepened, not because he suffered but *because he loved through it all.* And, remarkably, we come closer to accepting the previously paralyzing fear of our own pain and mortality. By vicariously entering into the moments of his life when he faced his greatest ordeals, we come to understand how Jesus could tolerate the loneliness of his ordeal and the agony of his death. We also may realize that redemptive suffering contains its own antidote to pain, and that loving *in spite of the consequences* converts our emotional and physical pain into a "passion"—or a complete surrender in service to the good—that has healing and redemptive power.

Conventional Christianity tells us that Jesus took on his suffering as a way to atone for our waywardness. Regardless of whether he accepted his suffering as a substitute sacrifice for our sins, or as a statement about his uncompromising commitment to loving—or both—it makes sense that this kind of sacrificial loving sends out a beacon that assists others in their spiritual journey.

In several of the encounters with Mary that I have obtained, Mary subtly encourages the recipient to embrace a willingness to suffer so that good can prevail. She exhibits a tremendous caring for those who face approaching physical or emotional hardship, or who are already undergoing an ordeal of some kind. But instead of alleviating the conditions under which the recipient labors, she invites them to surrender their sense of victimization and to embrace love above all else. In these encounters, Mary's presence brings a sense of meaning to situations that might otherwise provoke a sense of hopelessness or victimization. The recipient, meanwhile, enters a period of testing, in which the newly awakened qualities that Mary represents are challenged and seasoned by real-life circumstances. In these accounts, we can see a mature spirituality emerging—through meaningful suffering—even though the struggles leave the recipients often wondering if, by chance, they have taken a wrong turn in life.

Of all possible thankless tasks, parenting an adolescent may take the prize. We may laugh about it before and afterward, but while it is going on, it can be a nightmare. It brings its own form of suffering, for there often seems to be nothing we can do to prevent our relationships with them from deteriorating, at best, into an uneasy silence. As tensions escalate, we easily erupt over the smallest infraction because we interpret their thoughtlessness and distractibility as a lack of respect for us. We are often right about this, but no matter how correct we may be, we are sometimes wrong: On occasion we lash out and accuse them unfairly, wounding their emerging pride and losing their respect, deservedly. We drift apart, and yet desperately yearn for a time when we can fully reaffirm the love that was once so evident between us.

One woman, who was raising her adolescent children alone, felt she was losing all control over them. Without having a clue about what to do, she prayed to Mary instead.

The most profound experience I had with Mary took place near Akron, Ohio, where I lived at the time. About fifteen years ago, my children were in their late teens. Drugs— mostly marijuana—were very common in the schools they were attending. They were getting into "heavy metal" music, and they seemed different to me. It was hard to talk to them and get them to listen to reason. They were at an age when the opinions of their peers were more important than anything I could say to them.

I was very upset and did not know what to do. I was a divorced mother of four and had no support from their father. Also, I really felt alone in my need for some kind of religious influence. Although my children had all gone to church and Sunday school while growing up, they had since drifted away from attending and were not even remotely interested in returning to church.

One day while I was out driving around the countryside, I decided to visit St. Mary's, Ohio, which is about fifteen miles outside of Akron. The whole town is built around a beautiful old country church, and there is a grotto there in a cave that is a replica of Lourdes. In the summertime, all of the services are held outside where worshipers can sit in a parklike setting.

Even though I'm not Catholic, St. Mary's was always one of my favorite places to go when I was troubled, because the church was always open. So on that day, while the children were all in school, I went there and entered the grotto. Nobody else was there, even though there were candles burning.

I sat down. Up above the grotto, a ledge supported a statue of Mary. Someone had placed a lei of gladiolus around Mary's neck. It was absolutely beautiful. I sat there praying and talking to Mary, asking her what I should do about my children. I said, "You know, you're a mother—you know how these things should go."

All at once I felt a hand on my shoulder. I'd been sitting there for a while, and I thought it might be a priest. I turned around and saw no one. I looked around to see what this could be, and I felt this warmth even though it was a crisp day. I felt a warm glow enveloping me as I continued to feel the hand on my shoulder. I then noticed the birds had stopped singing, and everything had become very quiet.

I looked around and couldn't see anyone. Then the warm glow came over me again. It started slowly at the top of my head and worked down—down to the tip of my toes. Then I heard this voice in my ear say, "Don't worry, everything is going to be all right." *The voice—calm and beautiful—said,* "Raise your eyes and look at me." *So I looked up at the statue and saw a glow coming off the statue in gold, pulsating rays as if it was a living energy.*

One part of me was in awe, believing; and the other analytical part of me was asking, How can this be? I realized that the sun was behind the grotto and could not illuminate the enclosure. I kept looking and it kept pulsating and glowing. It moved around. And then I looked at the coral, pinkish gladiolus around her neck. They started glowing, too—but in a more bluish or purplish manner. I heard a commotion as though people were coming.

Then I saw a procession of light beings walking up the path! They were of different sizes, as though they were a family of light beings. They were just moving along toward the statue of Mary, and I wondered what was going to happen when they arrived. Eventually they reached the front of the grotto where the candles were. I saw that as they got there, the gold rays emanating from Mary began to extend outward to greet the family. Eventually the swirls from Mary absorbed and engulfed the little group. The glow continued and increased until I could see threads of light that were pulsating and waving and suffusing the statute in a golden glow.

While I watched, the sensation of the hand on my shoulder persisted. I wondered what to do and again I heard the voice say, "Be in peace. Everything is all right." *So I bowed my head and prayed to God and Mary. I surrendered my fears about the choices that my children were making.*

When I came out of meditation, I became aware that the singing of the birds had resumed. It was no longer so quiet. I raised my eyes and realized that the statue and flowers had lost their glow while I had been praying and meditating. Meanwhile, the feeling of the hand on my shoulder was also gone. Even so, I felt such an overwhelming sense of peace that I knew everything was going to be all right. My obsessive worry gave way to a profound feeling of peace.

When I got back to Akron, I noticed that my children acted more peacefully, probably because they sensed my inner change. It was a turning point for all of us.

I never lost the sense of peace that came upon me that day. Even today—fifteen years later—I remain much more peaceful because of the experience at St. Mary's. I was so impressed with this experience that I had a friend, who was a professional photographer, return to the grotto with me and take several pictures of the statue. She mounted one of them for me. Since then, the photo has always occupied a prominent place wherever I have lived. Whenever I see it, I am reminded of the glow that appeared from nowhere and brought my family a peace that we had lost. (P.W.)

In her encounter with a radiant Mary, P.W. witnesses what was evidently a spiritualized expression of her own family coming under the influence of her protective embrace. P.W. apprehends a view of her family that reminds her that we are spiritual beings—capable at any time of receiving healing and renewal through our connection with the Spirit. The concept of family takes on new meaning when one can experience, as P.W. did, the common spirit that unites us and resolves our apparent irreconcilable differences.

P.W.'s suffering gave way to a new response to her children borne of the peace that the experience with Mary instilled or restored in her. Her emotional struggle was alleviated by responding in a new way to a situation that drives innumerable parents into impotent fits of righteousness—and their children into full-scale defiance.

As I have already said, we can reasonably assume that her willingness to serve God's plan brought Mary the highest joy and the deepest suffering. Thus it makes sense that her example, if not her essence, dwells within each of us as a sobering reminder that the highest spiritual path can be, at times, a path of heartbreaking grief, as well. Given what Mary has come to mean to us, her manifestation at a time of personal difficulty can dramatically offset our human tendency to interpret pain as an indication that we have done something wrong. When she comes, we can take heart that our suffering may coincide with an important unfolding process whose overall purpose may remain somewhat obscure to us.

The following encounter with Mary took place during childbirth and was at once a blessing and an indication of coming trials.

I am most happy to write to you regarding my experience with the Blessed Mother. In fact, I thank you for the privilege and honor to do so. I have never written of this experience before. In fact, it was with great trepidation that I would even "speak" of it. As you well know, back in 1953, these experiences were regarded as hallucinations rather than actual encounters.

I was in great labor with my first-born child, J.D., on October 5, 1953. I remembered my dearly departed aunt

Lucille advising me to say the rosary during this time. I did so, over and over again.

My child was birthing himself when the nurse stopped him from coming into the world until I could be wheeled into the delivery room. I was given no drugs: It was a natural birth. As I was giving birth, I looked up and saw the Blessed Virgin. She was wearing a pure white mantilla that was flowing down, and a beautiful pale blue dress. She was absolutely beautiful. *I was awestruck. I couldn't tell the nun next to me, or anyone, in the delivery room she was there.* I could not speak. *The total beauty, tranquility, and serene feeling that engrossed my whole being still eludes me for an explanation. I still cannot describe it. Such peace, such beauty is beyond words. Seeing the Blessed Mother was so awe inspiring that I cannot to this day express the beauty of such a fantastic "sight and feeling."*

My son was born with a beautiful halo of golden hair about his head. As you may know, this can mean that the person will face great hardship in life. This has definitely been true for my son, and his ordeal continues to this day. I pray daily for him. May Mary, in her mercy, shine once more on her anointed one and lead him to the path of righteousness.

I thank you kindly for this opportunity to express my encounter with the mother of Jesus. (P.M.)

P.M. did not realize at the time of her vision that hardship was coming, and experienced the vision as entirely joyful and ineffably beautiful. Upon retrospect, however, she saw that Mary had come to awaken a sense of inner strength and spiritual presence that would serve to ease the burden of her grief over her son's troubles.

I asked P.M. what she meant by her son's ordeal. She said that he is a homosexual and has expressed many times his loneliness and despair over not being able to have his own children to love. He also struggles with a less ambiguous problem—alcoholism, a disease that runs in his family. Apparently, Mary saw fit to bless mother and son before the onset of a lifelong ordeal that, from a superficial standpoint, might seem tragic and unnecessary. However, if one accepts the near-death vision of Betty Eadie,[34] then P.M.'s assessment makes perfect sense. In Eadie's vision, she understood that souls enter life for a singular purpose: *to help others awaken.* At one point, Eadie even witnessed from her celestial point of view a drunk lying in a gutter. She knew that the soul had elected to experience alcoholism so that he could serve as an awakening influence for another soul who, as a physician, would come to treat his affliction. It seems like an unnecessary and uneconomical sacrifice from one point of view; but from where she stood, however briefly, Eadie knew the eventual awakening of awareness and love was all that really mattered.

When a serious disease strikes a person we love, we yearn for a miracle. Knowing that miracles can happen, we might pray for intervention, knowing that while we may feel unworthy ourselves, our loved ones deserve the very best.

Six years ago I moved to Virginia from New York. I had been in Virginia Beach six months when I received a letter from my younger sister. In the letter she painfully told me that she believed she had been infected with the AIDS virus and that she was already experiencing some of the symptoms. Needless to say, I was in shock since my sister had been in a monogamous relationship for eight years. I offered her an airplane ticket to Virginia Beach and said that together we would go for a test.

The test came back positive. The amount of pain that we experienced was unbelievable. My husband and I offered her and her two boys our home. We wanted to approach this situation with alternative medicine and with Edgar Cayce's remedies. This happened in November.

At that time, I was doing some volunteer work with a prayer group and made a very special friend. I confided my situation to her. She mentioned a promise made by Mary to the three children at Fatima. She promised that if you ask her anything on December 8 at noon, she will grant your wish. So on that day, my sister, my friend, and I prayed to Mary for my sister's health. Nothing happened to either one of us except that a sense of peace came over me.

That Christmas we all went to New York to spend the holidays with the rest of the family. My in-laws were living in New Jersey at that time, so my husband and I stayed over at their house. On Christmas Eve, my family and I spent the evening in New York and then went back to New Jersey late that night. That night I dreamt Mary came and blessed my sister.

In the dream, my sister and I were inside this building that had arched windows. To our left were many rows of chairs filled with people dressed in white. I believed they were doctors. Then, suddenly from one of the windows light came in and started to approach the doctors. The light turned to us, and as it was getting closer I saw the Virgin Mary appear in the light. The closer it got, the more clearly I saw her.

She stood in front of us. She smiled at us and touched my sister on the head. Then she turned away from us toward the window and rapidly left the room. As she left the room, I ran behind her and in my dream I asked, "If this is not a dream, please give me a sign." When I looked out the window, the sky had turned in all the variations of mauve, violet, lavender, and blue. Then lights lit up the entire sky as if they were fireworks. The clouds started to take shapes. I saw shapes of angels with trumpets announcing God's presence, and I think I saw what I believe was God, my beloved creator.

I woke up in tears as I'm now writing this to you.

My sister is still alive, battling this disease the best she can. We are grateful that she is still alive and know that God's presence is within us. I don't know what's going to happen to her, but I know that she will be all right, regardless.

One more thing. When we were children, my sister and I used to sing to Mary on December 8. On this day in my home country, we celebrate our beloved Mary with singing and sharing of food and sweets. It is a very important celebration for us. When we came to the U.S., we lost all that, that is, until we called out to her again with our prayers. (E.K.)

Shocked and overcome with emotional pain, E.K. set about to help her sister open herself to spiritual healing, and her remarkable experience seems to indicate that Mary intervened in the matter. However, it is clear from her account that Mary's apparent intervention did not heal E.K.'s sister once and for all. If she fails to recover, then we are left with the question: What's the point? What purpose does the vision serve if not to heal the affliction?

If we must all suffer and die as part of being human, then obviously it becomes a matter of how we *live* in the meantime that makes all the difference. *Feeling deeply loved can make all the difference in how we live.* Mary's loving presence may not prolong life in every case, but it may effectively forestall the sense of despair and meaninglessness that stalks us during our darkest hours. It is easy to imagine that Jesus felt his mother's love as he prayed alone on that last night.

In our struggle to understand why Mary's presence does not heal us outright—or at least grant a reprieve from suffering—we might consider other factors that might determine whether her intervention promotes healing of the body along with the undeniable impact on the soul. In several instances of healing in the New Testament, the afflicted persons had to do something in order to complete the process initiated by Jesus. On one occasion, Jesus told the lepers to go tell the priests that they had been healed, and only as they did so did they realize that they had been healed (Luke 17:11–19). In another instance, Jesus told a man who had been blind from birth that he had to go wash the mud from his eyes before his vision could be restored.

> *When he had said this, he spat on the ground and made mud with the saliva and spread the mud on the man's eyes, saying to him, "Go, wash in the pool of Siloam"* (John 9:6–7).

Only after complying with the Master's command did the blind man discover that he could see. So one question we might ask following an intervention from Mary or Jesus is, What am I called to do to continue the process that they have begun?

Another reason that the outcome of a Marian encounter may remain indeterminate has to do with the limitations of her mediational role, at least as it is defined by centuries of Catholic theology and mystical speculation: The church regards her as the *mediator* of grace, not its source. She is our advocate to Christ, who then may or may not "consent to be moved" by his mother's request.[35]

The tradition that Mary advocates for our needs when Christ might otherwise refuse "to be moved" has its roots in the account of the wedding at Cana. It was there that Mary asked Jesus to supply wine for the wedding feast.

> *When the wine gave out, the mother of Jesus said to him, "They have no wine." And Jesus said to her, "Woman, what concern is that to you and to me? My hour has not yet come." His mother said to the servants, "Do whatever he tells you"* (John 2:3–5).

His resistance and her quiet persistence give us an intimate view of their relationship, and how it may have worked to balance Jesus' vision of his future role with Mary's here-and-now human concerns. Her focus was on the immediate needs of those around her, while his was on the purpose of his life and the appropriate timing for revealing this purpose to others.

In some of the well-known apparitions, Mary's communications support this traditional view of her circumscribed, but nonetheless essential, role in bringing Christ's healing power into the lives of those who suffer. For instance, in the apparition at Pellevoisin, France, in 1876, Mary actually admitted not knowing whether the visionary, Estelle Faguette, would survive her illness. As Estelle lay dying of tuberculosis of the lung and bone, Mary appeared at the foot of her bed and told her that she wanted Estelle to spread her glory abroad if she lived through five more days of suffering. Estelle heard her say:

"Fear nothing! You know very well that you are my daughter. Courage! Be patient. My son consents to be moved. You will suffer another five days in honor of the five wounds of my Son. On Saturday, you will be either dead or cured. If my Son gives you back life, I want you to spread abroad my glory." [36]

As we are accustomed to thinking of such beings as all-knowing, we might puzzle at the fact that Mary could only assure Estelle of the *possibility* of her recovery. We are left to believe that the process hinged entirely on Jesus' will, which Mary could not command. Through Estelle's vision, we experience Mary as the mediator, much as she was at the wedding at Cana.

It is clear in these accounts that Mary knows Jesus, but she does not command him. In such stories, neither Jesus nor Mary emerges as a mere extension of the other, and by implication the unity between them is constantly reaffirmed by consent. Of course, this is how "real" relationships function well: They preserve each person's freedom to choose. If Mary and Jesus appeared to us as one spiritual being with a single voice, then there would be no relationship between them that could inform us about the virtues of cooperation, love, and sacrifice that we, as humans, extol so highly in our relationships.

We have seen how Mary's love can strengthen us to face difficulties of which we may be unaware at the time of her appearance. Unaware that her mother would soon become seriously ill, a woman experienced a vision of Mary in an orb of light.

If I may be allowed, I would like to share an experience I had. Although it occurred almost twenty years ago, it has remained as powerful and influential an experience as if it were happening now.

I was on the edge of a cornfield just at the entrance to a forest. I loved that hidden corner, where I went often to sit on the earth, surrender my cares, and "melt" into all being, so to speak. This particular time, I felt a presence just above me, so I raised my eyes. As I did so, it seemed as if my whole consciousness—indeed, my whole being—was raised to a higher level, as if vibrations became conscious, or I of them. There was an incredible buzzing sound, and I was intensely aware of the rapid vibrations of absolutely everything. It was as if everything was vibrating at a very high speed.

On a tree branch just above me, I saw a circle of light begin to form. The light concentrated more and more while at the same time radiating outward. Then in the center of that light I saw Mary. She was small and she moved along the branch toward me. The power and intensity of the apparition were phenomenal, so much so that my mind and being could not contain the experience. Mary hovered on or just above the branch for a few seconds, and then either she disappeared or my mind snapped out of a level of being able to attune to her. Seconds later a deer came out of the woods (I had never seen a deer there) and came very close to me before darting away.

I was left limp yet totally awed by the majesty and power of this visitation, which I knew in the core of my being was directly from the Higher Realms. My body shook with amazement, fear, and ecstasy. I was afraid—not of Mary, who was so unconditionally loving while being omniscient— but of the power of the energy. I knew if I were not "insulated" by my openness to her, so to speak, I would have burnt up right then and there.

A few months later my mother was diagnosed with very advanced stages of cancer, and my family was plunged into the agony of her suffering and of having to shift our entire worldview. It was then I knew why Mary had come to me. She had come to protect me, to be a comfort and reassuring essence, to pour love into me as I went through a terribly, terribly shattering phase of my life.

Since that experience, Mary has come to me often. She has never returned as an outer vision; rather, she appears to me in times of meditation or visualization. Any time I need a nurturing, loving, completely understanding presence, she is there for me. I trust she is here always and will be my guide and companion whenever I am desperate, confused, or terribly unsure. I feel absolutely sure that everyone is under the wings of her love and protection, and I feel very blessed to know this consciously. (A.T.)

A.T.'s experience with Mary confirms that while her presence instills a lasting sense of peace, the gift is often commensurate with the challenges ahead. Just as so many people report receiving a financial windfall just prior to unanticipated losses, it is as if Mary comes to prepare us and insulate us against the loss of hope that could easily befall us at times of crisis and despair.

This remarkable encounter with Mary parallels the reports of many of the well-known apparition visionaries who typically describe an electrified atmosphere and a radical shift in awareness just prior to Mary's actual appearances. The children at Fatima heard a clap of thunder before they saw her approach in a cloud of light and settle near the branch of a tree. The power of her presence is a well-recognized feature of Marian encounters.

My own limited experience bears this out. For instance, I once dreamt I was with two friends, and we suddenly realized that Mary was about to appear. As we watched a particular place where we believed she would manifest, I felt my mind suddenly open up to her. The atmosphere around us became electrified, and the influx of her love and power was nearly overwhelming. As she began to appear to us, I cried out in joy. And then I awakened, knowing that I probably would have seen her if I had remained silent! Nevertheless, I experienced communion with her for a moment, and such moments I shall always treasure.

People who are unfulfilled in their marriages may eventually consider the question of whether to stay and make the best of it or to end the relationship. With few legal and societal obstacles to divorce, many opt to follow the dream of a better life on our own or with someone new. Ultimately, ending a marriage can be a very lonely and difficult decision. The contributor of the following account knew this all too well.

The last line of the song "My Rosary" reads "to strive at last to learn to kiss the cross." That line captures an almost fatalistic willingness to accept the will of God. In 1956, I had an experience which gave me an opportunity to do so.

It was March, and a stormy March at that, when my wife and I began having sexual problems due to her illness. We were on the verge of breaking up when I was practically forced to accept an out-of-town job.

One stormy night, I had gone to bed when an area-wide power failure occurred. Not knowing this, I awoke to find my room flooded with light. I looked around and saw our Blessed Mother, half seated on the low dresser beside my bed. She was dangling a long rosary from her right hand, with the crucifix lying on the backs of her fingers.

Not really believing my eyes, I propped myself up on one elbow, but the vision was still there. She never spoke a word. She merely extended her hand. I was somehow directed to kiss the cross, and I did. Then she smiled—a benediction—and disappeared. The light was gone, too. Needless to say, I found sleep very difficult. I lay awake and thought about what had happened.

I would have dismissed the whole thing as a dream, except for one thing. The next morning the owner of the hotel stopped me as I came down the stairs and asked me about the brilliant light in my room. Doubly shaken, I told him it had to be my electric lantern, and he was satisfied with that. He had been on the street asking a utility crew how long the blackout would last, and he had seen my room ablaze with light.

It happened that the job finished in a few days, so I returned home—without any notion of separation. For almost thirty years I nursed my wife after that night, but at last she died.

That event changed my whole life. From that night, I have remained a dedicated servant of those who need help. I do not do this in an organized fashion: I simply serve those whom I encounter in my everyday life. To these people, I have dedicated my whole being. I give without thought of recompense. I just give. (C.H.)

C.H.'s response to Mary's offer of the cross was twofold: to accept the hardship of his relationship and to experience the joy of surrendering to a path of service. Consequently, he apparently remained free of the regret and resentment that often accompanies a decision to remain in a difficult relationship.

We might conclude that Mary appeared to C.H. to encourage him to remain in his marriage. Perhaps so. However, his willingness to kiss the cross might signify a more important and fundamental commitment. His act of submission may have cemented a relationship *with Christ through Mary* that, from that moment, superseded any other relationship, including his marriage. From this point of view, his compliance with Mary's invitation bound him to Christ but freed him to choose his course in life without risking the loss of his relationship with God. By the same token, it empowered him to undertake willingly a difficult course of action that may have seemed excessively self-sacrificing from a less spiritually committed point of view.

In Catholic theology, Mary always points to Christ and stands just below him in the heavenly hierarchy as our advocate before him. But on another level, she gives us something from herself, as well—her own unique *experience* that can inspire us and console us as we experience the heights and depths of earthly life. In the following encounter, we can see how her *empathy*, borne of her own experience, can foster healing during times of our greatest losses.

I lost my father one year and one day ago. Since then, I have prayed the rosary more devoutly, but I recited it weekly with a group prior to my loss. As part of my Catholicism, it is customary to offer up one's Holy Communion for a departed loved one or for those souls in purgatory. So, on one occasion, I was in line to receive communion. I was third in line, and a statue of Mary stood off to my left. As I silently offered to my father the communion I was about to receive, I heard very

clearly an aged woman's voice say, "I lost someone, too.
I lost my son."

*At that very moment, it was my turn to receive
communion, and my eyes looked upon Jesus on the cross. I
knew then who had spoken to me.*

*Several days later, as I prayed the rosary over my daddy's
grave, I saw tears falling on the grave marker—and they
were not mine.* (K.C.)

As Mary comes to us—in our own experiences or through the
heart-opening accounts of others—it may seem surprising that she
holds out a cross for us to kiss, or a grief to be remembered. But
through her presence, we learn that suffering has a place in our
development, just as it had a place in her life as the mother of Jesus.
We, too, apparently must learn that there is always something to
take up, and always something to give up, before we can fully accept
the greater destiny that awaits us.

Consecration Prayer
to the Immaculate Heart of Mary

Oh, Most Pure Heart of Mary,
full of goodness,
show your love toward us.
Let the flame of your heart, O Mary,
descend on all people.
We love you immensely;
impress on our hearts true love
so that we long for you.
Oh, Mary, gentle and humble of heart,

remember us when we sin.
You know that all people sin.
Grant that through your most pure and motherly heart
we may be healed from every spiritual sickness.
Grant that we may always experience
the goodness of your motherly heart
and that through the flame of your heart
we may be converted.

Fatima

T HE SERIES OF APPARITIONS AT FATIMA, Portugal, in 1917 took place during a time of political upheaval and war. Religious meeting had been abolished by the Portuguese government, and the country verged on totalitarianism. Elsewhere, the First World War raged in Europe. So the conditions were ripe for an intervention that would, at once, warn and inspire the faithful to pray for the necessary changes in the world.

Three children—Lucia de Santos, and her cousins Francisco and Jacinta Marto—were tending cattle one day when Lucia saw a translucent cloud in the shape of a human body float overhead and hover above a pine grove. That was all she saw. A whole year passed before the children were again watching over some cattle, and they were greeted by a strange wind and the sight of the cloud that Lucia had seen the year before. This time, the cloud approached them and revealed itself to be a young man, who identified himself as the Angel of Peace. He bowed and prayed the same simple prayer three times, and then urged the children to pray likewise: *"My God,*

I believe, I adore, and I love you! I beg pardon of you for those who do not believe, do not adore, do not hope, and do not love you!" Then the angel vanished.

The children decided not to tell anyone about their vision, fearing ridicule from their friends and family. Lucia, in particular, was most adamant in insisting on keeping the encounter a secret, because she had been humiliated on an earlier occasion when she had been overheard confessing to her priest.

The angel appeared to them again on two more occasions. During his final visit, he administered the host to Lucia and then offered the chalice to all three children. Again, he repeated a prayer three times before leaving them.

The children continued to pray and make whatever sacrifices they could. Then, on May 13, 1917, Mary herself appeared to them. As they were moving their flocks to the meadows of the Cova de Iria, they were startled by a bright flash. Thinking it was lightning, they ran for the nearest cover. Then they saw a bright orb hovering over a nearby evergreen tree. In the middle of the light they could see a woman dressed in white, holding a rosary. Then she spoke to them in a melodious voice: *"Don't be afraid, I won't hurt you!"*

Lucia then asked the Lady where she came from, to which she replied, *"I am from heaven."*

Hearing this, Lucia asked the Lady what she wanted. The Lady replied, *"I come to ask you to come here for six months in succession, on the thirteenth day at this same hour. Then I will tell you who I am, and what I want. And afterward I will return here a seventh time."*

After more questions, the Lady asked, *"Do you wish to offer yourselves to God, to endure all the suffering that he may please to send you, as an act of reparation for the sins by which he is offended, and to ask for the conversion of sinners?"*

The children replied, "Yes, we do." The Lady then told them that they would have much to suffer, but that God's grace would be their comfort.

After having such astounding experiences, the children felt increased pressure to tell others about what they had seen. Jacinta finally let it slip that the children had seen a "pretty lady" at the Cova de Iria. Even though many of the adults expressed initial skepticism, soon everyone believed that the children had seen the Blessed Mother.

The beautiful lady kept her promise by appearing to the children on the thirteenth of the month for the next six months. During the July visitation, she gave them three secrets to keep until further notice, and promised that a miracle would take place during the final apparition which would help everyone believe that she had, indeed, appeared to the children.

Meanwhile, the local authorities were so incensed by the attention that the apparitions were drawing, and by the fact that the children would not reveal the nature of the secrets, that the mayor kidnapped the children just prior to the August apparition date, threw them in jail, and threatened to execute them.

The local townspeople, unaware that the children had been kidnapped, showed up for the August visitation. Even though the children were not there, they reported seeing various supernatural phenomena, such as a cloud that appeared around the tree where the apparitions had occurred, and a clap of thunder that seemed to come from underground.

During the last apparition, on October 13, 1917, the Lady revealed herself to be our Lady of the Rosary. Seventy thousand witnesses saw the sun spin out of its orbit, emitting a rainbow of color as it gyrated. Then they observed the sun plunging toward the earth, causing many of them to scream in terror. When the sun eventually returned to its place in the sky, many of these rain-soaked people found their clothing completely dry. Many of the crowd also reported experiencing healing, or an alleviation of their medical problems, following the stunning display. In addition, over ten thousand people in the surrounding villages witnessed the supernatural event from a distance.

It was not until 1942 that the first two secrets were revealed. In the first, the children beheld a vision of hell that was so terrible that it prompted them to devote themselves to praying for the redemption of sinners. In the second, the Blessed Mother told them that the First World War would end, but that a more horrible war would ensue if man did not change his ways. The conversion of Russia was apparently critical in preventing further world crises. The third secret has never been revealed by the church. Three popes have learned of it, but each of them has decided not to release it.

5

THE WAY OF
Surrender

Those who go on are the great and strong spirits,
who do not seek to know, but are driven to be.

Evelyn Underhill

IN ADDITION TO PHYSICAL AND EMOTIONAL
suffering, another kind of ordeal awaits many people who follow a
spiritual path. This form of suffering afflicts us most intensely
when, after having chosen to give ourselves more fully to God, we
are made aware of old attitudes and behaviors that compromise our
capacity to serve. While various character weaknesses may have
posed no particular impediment to us in the past, they now threaten
to undermine the more exacting commitment that we have made. In
response to our need to become aware of and resolve these
disabling attitudes and behaviors, Jesus and Mary may come to us

as loving but stern taskmasters who challenge us to let go of much of what we once considered acceptable.

When we are called by the Spirit to do more with our lives, it seems that a host of messengers confronts us with the ways that we have compromised our highest ideals. Virtually everyone seems intent on "weighing us in the balance and finding us wanting." This seemingly endless wake-up call can feel like punishment; but the painful process brings blessings in disguise, for the confrontational process helps us to face and resolve the issues that stand squarely between us and a more complete acceptance of our spiritual calling. Some rare individuals are, presumably, ready to give up everything in their quest for spiritual communion and wholeness. Consequently, they face very little of the struggle that faces those of us who hold on to our old ways. But most of us do not go gently into that process of spiritual surrender. As C. S. Lewis said, we hold back and relate to our spiritual calling like a good man who pays his taxes. "He pays them all right, but he does hope there will be enough left over for him to live on." Lewis points out that the spiritual life is much harder and much easier than that: "Christ says, 'Give me all.' "[37]

In many of the encounters with Mary that I have obtained in my research, the recipient not only encounters Mary "out there" but enters a process of imitating, internalizing, and incorporating her being within themselves. As they move toward a full identification with her, they also must face and resolve the barriers to this trans-formation, usually in the form of unacknowledged, self-limiting beliefs and fears. In the encounters in this chapter and the next, we will vicariously experience what it is like to be asked by Mary to face and surrender these limitations. We will see this process continue in the next chapter to the point where the recipients can reasonably say that Mary now lives within them, through them—and even *as* them.

When Jesus called the disciples, he presumably did so with a full knowledge of their weaknesses and faults. Still, he chose to teach them and, eventually, to commission them to do his work. When we consider how he chose these men *in spite* of their faults, we have to wonder what it was about them that informed Jesus that they could serve him anyway. What informed Christ that Paul, for that matter, could become the disciple that he did? We might ask, as well, if something within ourselves overshadows the limitations that otherwise stand in the way of serving him.

A man who had been unfaithful to his wife throughout his twenty years of marriage—and who had rejected God throughout—turned to Mary and the rosary out of sheer desperation. After praying the rosary daily for three weeks, Christ came to him in spite of all that he had done to deny him.

> *I was raised in a very religious Roman Catholic home where devotion to the Blessed Mother was taught. As young children we would gather together at night to say the rosary with our mother.*
>
> *At the age of nine, I became an altar boy and eventually entered the seminary to study for the priesthood. Approximately a year prior to entering the seminary, my brother, who was fifteen years old at the time, died of leukemia after a three-week stay in a hospital. His death devastated me. There was no one closer to me, and to this day I still feel the pain of seeing him die in that hospital room. The following September I began my studies for the priesthood only to become more acutely depressed. As time went on*

I eventually left the seminary. With each day I became further depressed with the contemplation of suicide becoming more and more prevalent.

A year after leaving the seminary I entered undergraduate studies. Along with my depression came anger. I became more and more hostile toward God. I eventually abandoned the church and Mass and began to study Buddhism. My study and practice of Buddhism lasted over fifteen years. Meditation became a way of dealing with the overwhelming pain that existed within me. It was not God-centered but purely utilitarian.

During these years of consciously trying to eliminate God from my life, my saintly mother continued to poke and prod me into returning to church. On one such day, the fear of God was enough to cause me to return to praying the rosary. My praying continued for three weeks, at which point my life changed.

On this particular day I was walking through my home, which was empty except for myself. As I walked through the dining room, I was suddenly thrown to the floor, and I began to cry with an intensity beyond my understanding. I then heard a voice within me repeat very distinctly three times, "You can live your life any way you want, but you can no longer deny me." *I had the undeniable sense that I was hearing Jesus' voice. This shook me to my very core.*

I can't say exactly how long I remained on that floor or continued to cry, but the experience has remained the most profound and transforming incident of my life.

Needless to say, I was not leading an exemplary life by any means. The only part of my life that changed was the fact that I was praying the rosary.

Today I am eternally grateful to the Blessed Mother for her intercession before Jesus where she pleaded for my soul. I live with the truth that the mother of Jesus and her son love each and every one of us beyond our earthly understanding. I have no doubt that anyone who approaches Mary approaches God as well.

I hope that my experience may help others realize that there is truly a loving mother available to us in Mary, who carries us in her arms before Christ her son. (B.F.)

B.F.'s encounter with Christ takes him completely by surprise and leaves him with a clear mandate to change his life. The overwhelming authority of Christ remains, however, softened by his acceptance of B.F.'s freedom of choice. Indeed, he leaves B.F. free to do anything *except to deny him.* Perhaps Jesus recognized in B.F. —as he apparently did in Paul—a capacity to serve him in spite of the conscious choices he had made up to that point. Whether this capacity takes the form of a childlike heart or a penchant for radical honesty, it is likely that even the worst of us possess a redeeming quality that the Spirit can use in the furthering of love.

Of all the challenges that must have faced Mary in her lifetime, grief must rank near the top. Some people believe Mary knew so completely Jesus would rise from the dead that her suffering was minimal. Most of us, however, probably find it hard to imagine her experiencing anything other than the most severe, wrenching pain as she saw him die. In Catherine Emmerich's visions of the life of Mary, Emmerich, a nun who also experienced the stigmata during her life, observed Mary experiencing anguish for the rest of her life because she longed so much for reunion with him.[38]

Knowing that Mary probably suffered immensely, she comes to mind as someone whose encouragement to cease grieving would carry tremendous weight. For what better source of guidance can there be than one who has borne her ordeal with grace?

The woman who experienced the following encounter with Mary had become attached to a man who personified for her many of the attributes of Christ, and upon whom she became dependent as she poured out her pain and hopes in her letters to him.

I had been corresponding with M. for many months. Without realizing it, two things occurred within me that set me up for the rug getting pulled out from under me. I had developed a strong transference of my needs onto him. Also, confused with all I was experiencing, I was turning to him for help and guidance when I should have been turning to Jesus. It was really very selfish and a terrible thing to do to M., and I felt very sorry for it. In all fairness and with great respect, he was always gracious, generous, and patient with me.

The thing is, I am a very expressive individual. The Lord has given me many beautiful expressive gifts. But I have been like a caged and muted canary—always stifled and afraid to sing. But with M.'s gentleness and kindness— as well as the inspiration of his excellent writings—I felt safe and understood. I believed he was listening and that he cared. But with more than a thousand miles between us, as well as taking into consideration the unbalanced and confused state I was in, I was very out of touch with the reality of his situation or of the nature of our friendship. Eventually, he did the wise thing of saying "Enough is enough" and terminated our correspondence. I was very hurt and couldn't seem to stop crying.

So there I was weeping and weeping. It became chronic. The more I cried, the more it upset the balance of my already delicate state. I felt paper-thin and oddly disconnected from my body. I felt all control slipping away.

But then one morning in the wee hours I felt myself waking up. I was very lucid—that is, aware of the bed and the covers. But I was also aware that I was in an altered state of consciousness: There was a sweet, velvety feeling all through and around me. I found myself whispering aloud in a low tone, "Mary! Beautiful Mary!"

Then in my mind, I saw my typewriter. Then I saw the cover being placed over it, and then it being turned around backward. Next, I heard Mary say, "That's what women are made of—strength and fortitude." *It seemed that the experience was now over, and I lay quietly trying to comprehend what she had meant. But apparently, I didn't understand adequately, because I heard another voice say,* "She came to tell you to refrain from pining."

In looking up the meaning of "pining," I came to realize that it referred to my continual weeping and lamenting, but it also referred to a habitual way of relating to life. I often expect myself and my relationships to be perfect here and now; and when I or the relationship falls short, I agonize over it. I have found guidance in her message to me—both for the immediate situation regarding M., and in regard to a longstanding need to address this tendency to feel victimized. (K.F.)

Living in the world means eventually losing everything to which we cling. We like to avoid this sober realization as much as we can, but if we are honest with ourselves, it lurks behind every thought and feeling. In recognition of this heartbreaking truth, Mary has said to several visionaries that they will experience happiness in heaven but not on earth. With this succinct summation, Mary conveys what seems like a rather pessimistic, even fatalistic, view of earthly life from someone who might be in a position to make a difference. But if we accept that Mary and Jesus sacrificed much of what the world would consider desirable, even necessary, so that love could prevail, then why would they want less of us? Of course, religion that is based on salvation through faith, or vicarious atonement, is based on the idea that Christ's sacrifice frees us from having to atone for our own sins. But perhaps salvation *also frees us to do more* in difficult, challenging situations. Perhaps salvation also means choosing a meaningful—and perhaps difficult—life as fully as Jesus and Mary once did.

The plight of Lot's wife, who turned into a pillar of salt because she hesitated to follow God's directive, dramatizes the consequences of having accepted one's calling, only to hesitate in carrying it out. Indeed, nothing apparently provokes a more severe response from the Spirit than turning back on one's commitment. I have learned this lesson many times but still find occasions to waiver in my resolve. Three years ago, my wife and I were about to embark on a book promotional tour of a spiritual story I had written earlier in the year. Although I had written other books, this was my first self-publishing effort, and the story revolves around a vision of the Blessed Mother. After investing thousands of dollars and much of our time and energy, my doubts began to take hold.

We were sitting up in bed one night sincerely questioning our upcoming efforts to launch the book in my hometown area, two thousand miles from where we lived at the time. It was going to take a lot more energy and money than we had bargained for. Unable to fall asleep, I left the bedroom and went into the office. Meanwhile, Kathy lay in bed and began praying for Mary's assistance. This is what happened next:

Shortly after I began praying, I felt Mary's presence in the room. I soon fell asleep and began dreaming. Scott and I were preparing for our trip and discussing our concerns about the project, just as we had prior to my falling asleep. He went into the laundry room and called to me. I walked in and looked at the ceiling. There was a distinct presence there that I knew was Mary. Scott put his arm around me and we fell to our knees, very afraid. We were then raised off the floor and lifted toward the ceiling. While I never heard her speak, I sensed that she was conveying the message that if we were unwilling to honor our commitment and do the work we agreed to do, then our presence on the earth was no longer needed. I put my hand up to stop us from going through the ceiling. The feeling I had was that I wasn't ready to die, and that I would stay here and do the work I felt called to do.

Mary was not the comforting presence that I've felt before during other encounters. I felt she was chastising us and reminding us of who was really in charge of this work.

I woke myself up by calling out Scott's name. I lay in bed frightened and just wanted to go back to sleep. But then I felt a jolt of energy in my lower back, and I knew I had to get up to tell him about my dream vision.

I am glad to say that we went forward with a renewed commitment from that time. (K.R.S.)

In the following near-death encounter with Mary, we find that Mary responds much differently to another person's indecision. In this moving account, a woman faces a choice between the ultimate freedom that death affords her, and the task of staying alive and taking care of those she loves. Instead of chastising her for her ambivalence, Mary remains dispassionate throughout this encounter, allowing the woman to arrive at her own decision.

I was lying in my hospital bed—in extreme pain from an allergic reaction to a drug—when Mary appeared to me and motioned for me to follow her. She "spoke" to me without moving her lips—it was as if I could read her thoughts. I went to her and, looking down, I could see myself in the bed. At one moment I was in the bed, and the next moment I was floating above it. I could also see my husband sitting in a chair to the right of my bed. I had no emotional feeling toward "myself" in the bed, nor to my distraught husband in the chair.

I could also see all the rooms above the floor where I was located. I could see down the hallway and into the nursery, where my infant son slept. The view of the hospital floor was much like one sees when playing with a dollhouse: I saw no roof but several rooms separated by walls. I noticed the room across the hall from mine. It was a waiting room that contained a statue of Mary.

The minute I floated to Mary, I was no longer in pain. I felt nothing. Mary prompted me to follow her up a corridor which was filled with brilliant light and the most beautiful music. I felt completely at peace within myself and total love and unconditional acceptance from her.

The first thing I said to Mary was how very beautiful she was. She had the appearance of a young girl. She was dressed

*in a full-length gown with a blue piece that draped her head
and fell to her feet. Her feet were bare except for golden sandals.*

*As we continued up the corridor, I felt that we were going
to see God. The corridor made a sharp turn to the left. From
this angle I could see that the light was even more brilliant
and the love which flowed down was stronger than any I have
ever encountered. Just before we reached the angle, I told Mary,
"No, wait. I can't go with you, I have two kids to care for."*

Mary stopped, turned to me, and said, "It will not be easy."

*I said, "I know, but I must go back." At that very instant,
I was back in my body, again racked with the terrible pain.*

*Mary was indeed right: My life was not easy for many
years. I experienced recurring nightmares about the medical
experience and replayed the near-death encounter. I carried
extreme guilt around with me because I had not been
concerned about "leaving" my husband to go with Mary, as
I had my two kids.*

*For years I was afraid to share my encounter with
anyone lest they consider me crazy. I agonized over being
"special" as only very special people in the Catholic church's
history had been blessed by encounters with Mary. I became
aware much later that we are all special. But I couldn't
understand at first why I had had the encounter.*

*I later understood that the encounter was meant to bring
me comfort at a very stressful time in my life and that I could
convey that same comfort to others by sharing my encounter.*
(T.A.)

On the surface, Mary seems insensitive to T.A.'s struggle about
whether to leave her children and husband behind. Her apparent

aloofness seems strange, given the compassion and motherliness that we associate with the Blessed Mother. But by remaining aloof, Mary allows T.A. to arrive at a decision that *she alone* must bear. Mary's words, *It will not be easy,* should not surprise us or make us think that T.A. had chosen wrongly. For, in all of the apparitions, and in all of the personal encounters with her that we have considered, no one has ever heard Mary say that doing the right thing would be easy.

How can we reconcile Mary's anger in Kathy's dream with her aloofness in T.A.'s near-death encounter? Clearly, Kathy and I were considering breaking a commitment that we had already made. From various biblical passages, we know that God deals harshly with broken promises. T.A., in contrast, faced a decision that seemed altogether new, occasioned by her imminent passage from this life. From these two contrasting experiences, it seems correct to say that as we choose, the Spirit becomes a partner in that choice and aligns itself with us in covenants that cannot be easily broken. We become less free in one sense, but then again, we are never quite as alone as before. From the moment of our consent, we have a silent partner who is very much invested in the fulfillment of our promise.

In the following account, another woman, A.T., makes a decision to "live through" an ordeal without distancing herself from the feelings that engulfed her at the time.

When my niece died unexpectedly at age ten, my family fell apart. It was a very upsetting time for us, and everyone seemed to react by trying to deny their grief, to block it out, and to "soldier ahead." I was simply too overwhelmed by grief to shut out my feelings, so what happened was that

I was carrying the grief for the entire family. I was quite unstable as my family found it necessary to attack me to keep their own feelings locked up. I remember feeling so terribly vulnerable and wobbly then, yet from somewhere an incredible feminine energy came to me and kept reassuring me. I was told by this presence to stay fully present and aware of my feelings. I knew I had to do my grieving in a "feminine" way—that is, by walking through the awful ordeal and embracing the earthiness of it versus cutting it off and "soldiering ahead," the masculine way. This reassuring voice and energy kept coming to me telling me that it was okay and that someday I would get through the pain and move on, as I have. (A.T.)

By shouldering this burden fully, A.T. brings grace into an otherwise unbearable experience of loss. As such, she imitates Mary, whose whole life we associate with a willingness to bring the Divine into the human heart under the most heartbreaking conditions imaginable.

From these stories, we learn that we are called upon to put aside our fears and resistances and to give more of ourselves than ever before. They invite us, not so much to *transcend* our limiting circumstances, but to *enter into life more completely* with a depth of openness and love that, paradoxically, frees us from the pain and constraints that we would ordinarily avoid.

Indeed, this form of suffering contains within it its own antidote—a recognition of the meaningfulness of our ordeal, and an unfolding relationship with two beings who embraced the heights and depths of human experience as an acceptable and necessary part of loving.

Hail, Holy Queen

Hail, Holy Queen, Mother of Mercy,
our life, our sweetness and our hope!
To thee do we cry, poor banished children of Eve;
to thee do we send up our sighs,
mourning and weeping in this valley of tears!
Turn then, most gracious Advocate,
thine eyes of mercy towards us,
and after this, our exile,
show unto us the blessed fruit of thy womb, Jesus.
O clement, O loving, O sweet Virgin Mary!
Pray for us, O Blessed Mother of God,
that we may be made worthy of the promises of Christ.

Garabandal

I N JUNE 1961, IN THE NORTHWESTERN SPANISH
village of San Sebastian de Garabandal, four young girls—Mari-
Loli Mazon (twelve), Jacinta Gonzalez (twelve), Maria Cruz Gonzalez
(eleven), and Conchita Gonzalez (twelve)—were stealing apples
from their schoolteacher's orchard, when suddenly they heard a
sound like thunder, and an angel appeared. Although the angel said
nothing and soon disappeared, the girls—who had been forced to
their knees in the angel's presence—were afraid that he had come to
punish them. They ran back to the village and told their friends and
families what they had witnessed. Over the next few days, the angel
reappeared to them on several occasions, remaining silent as before.
Then on July 1, he finally spoke, saying: *"Do you know why I have
come? It is to announce to you that tomorrow the Blessed Virgin will
appear to you as our Lady of Mount Carmel."*

The word spread, and on July 2, several visiting priests and
numerous villagers accompanied the girls to the spot where they
had first seen the angel. There the girls encountered the Blessed
Mother standing between two angels, both of whom looked like the
angel who had appeared to them previously. Above and to the right
of Mary was a large single eye, which they called the eye of God. In

subsequent appearances, Mary sometimes appeared with the infant Jesus in her arms.

The girls found it easy to speak with Mary during the first encounter. Conchita said it was like visiting with your mother after she had been away on a trip. Toward the end of the vision, Mary asked the girls to pray the rosary and taught them to say it correctly.

Over the next five years, Mary appeared to the girls on over two thousand occasions. In the tradition of the previous Marian apparitions, the Blessed Mother asked the visionaries to plead with humanity to engage in various spiritual practices to mitigate the effects of humanity's sinfulness. In one of the early apparitions, she revealed her principal message to the world:

> *"Many sacrifices must be made. Much penance must be done. We must pay many visits to the Blessed Sacrament . . . but first of all we must be very good. . . . If we do not do this, punishment awaits us . . . already the cup is filling, and if we do not change we shall be punished."*

The visionaries claimed that the Blessed Mother told them about a series of warnings that would take place in order to give humanity time to mend its ways. These events are supposed to include a worldwide warning that will be experienced by everyone on earth, a great miracle that will take place within a year after the first warning, and a permanent sign that will remain visible at Garabandal and other apparition sites. If the world fails to respond to these warnings, then a terrible chastisement will allegedly take place, during which as many as two-thirds of the people in the world will die.

In 1961, the bishop at Santander, Spain, appointed a commission to evaluate the apparitions. Although the commission concluded, "We have not found anything deserving of ecclesiastical censure or condemnation either in the doctrine or in the spiritual recommendations," it also stated that there was "no proof that the said apparitions, visions, locutions, or revelations can so far be presented as true and authentic."

In 1986, a new bishop, Bishop del Val Gallo—who had declared the message of Garabandal "important" and "theologically correct"—appointed another commission to evaluate the Garabandal apparitions. While the commission found the content of the messages consistent with the church's teachings, they had difficulty in establishing anything that could be considered "supernatural."

It may seem that the appointed commissions were unnecessarily negative in their assessments, but the church has been historically cautious about such claims. The thinking is: There are good angels and there are bad angels, and angels can influence the natural order in various "preternatural" ways. Unless the phenomena rise above the capacity of angels—and are clearly "supernatural"—then they are possibly of a demonic origin. The words *preternatural* and *supernatural* are very similar in meaning; that is, they both pertain to that which is outside of, or above the laws of nature. But the church refers to "supernatural" as something that can only originate in God.

In 1992, the new bishop of Santander, José Vilaplana, appealed to Rome for pastoral direction on the matter, and the Vatican responded that it saw no reason to overturn the conclusions of the earlier commissions. Nonetheless, the findings of the two commissions have recently been forwarded to the Holy See for review.

In the meantime, Catholics might do well to consider Colin Donovan's even-handed perspective on this matter: "It seems

. . . notwithstanding the decisions of two commissions accepted by the bishops of Santander, that there are reasonable grounds for individual Catholics to find Garabandal credible. . . . Given the seriousness of the times we do well to heed the message of conversion . . . with complete confidence in God's providence for us and the world. The future will take care of itself if we remain spiritually prepared for anything. This has always been the advice of the saints, anyway." [39]

6

A MODEL FOR
Us All

Mary's life is a rule of life for all.
Saint Ambrose

THE PRACTICE OF IMITATING OTHERS BEGINS EARLY
in life. Little girls dress up like their mothers and make a mess of
things just to feel what it's like to be a grownup. Little boys pin their
fathers' war medals on their chests so they can feel powerful in a
world where they are still, as yet, small and vulnerable. Through
this imaginative play, children do more than simply pretend: They
gradually become what they imitate.

Just because we grow up does not mean that the urge to imitate
others diminishes or becomes less important in our development.
As C. S. Lewis points out, these childlike impulses assist us in
growing up spiritually, as well.

Very often the only way to get a quality in reality is to start behaving as if you had it already. That is why children's games are so important. They are always pretending to be grownups—playing soldiers, playing shop. But all the time, they are hardening their muscles and sharpening their wits, so that the pretense of being grownup helps them to grow up in earnest.[40]

In many of the historic apparitions and personal encounters with Mary, she essentially invites us to imitate her. She urges us to love and to forgive others, to practice prayer and fasting, and to remain in constant adoration of Christ. Indeed, everything that she has given to us—through the biblical record, the well-known apparitions, and the personal visions we have considered herein—comprises, in essence, *a method of imitating her.* Some individuals, in particular, have embraced these methods and have embarked on a spiritual quest to imitate her, and to serve the one she serves. My friend, M.B., is one such person.

When I ran into her for the first time in over fifteen years, I told her about my research into Marian visions and dreams. As we parted, she quietly said that she would be willing to share some of her own experiences of Mary with me. Needless to say, I was eager to meet with her to hear her story. A few weeks later, we met in a cafe overlooking the Atlantic Ocean and talked about her experiences of encountering Mary on several separate occasions. As she finished talking, she said, "I feel Mary inside of me now. She is always with me."

As we have seen in the previous chapter, individuals who wish to enter into a relationship with Christ by imitating Mary must first face and resolve their resistances to a fuller relationship with the Divine. We will now consider a few individuals who, like M.B., may have already resolved the significant impediments to their internalization of, and identification with, the Holy Mother. Consequently, they have entered into a relationship with Mary in which she has become, as Saint Teresa of the Child Jesus once said, "more mother than queen"—and perhaps for some, even more friend than mother. Engaged in ongoing communion and identification with the Blessed Mother, they feel that *Mary now lives in them and through them as their own higher natures.* By becoming one with her, these individuals become wedded to the Christ Spirit within themselves, and channels of blessings in a variety of ways.

Of course, it is a daunting challenge to present their stories succinctly, for their entire lives—not just single dreams or visions—reflect their commitment to a co-creative relationship with God. And each richly moving story is not a simple thing to tell. Nevertheless, what follows are highlights from the lives of such individuals.

Among the rich dreams and prayer experiences that M.B. shared with me, she revealed a startling baptismal experience that she had disclosed to only a few close friends. She knew it was the kind of thing that most people would find hard to accept. But if her experience seems grandiose from one point of view, it is devastating from another. In essence, she experienced what it would have been like for her for *God to have passed her over in favor of Mary.* Here is her story in her own words.

> *I was raised Catholic, and at a very young age I felt an intense—even extraordinary—devotion to Mary. I participated in all of the church rituals related to Mary, and I regularly prayed the rosary. Even in later years—when I was no longer involved with the Catholic church—I still carried the rosary. Occasionally, I would even recite it.*
>
> *When I was exposed to the theory that Mary may have been a member of the Essene sect of Judaism, and may have*

actively prepared with other maidens to become the channel of the Christ child, she became the pattern that I chose for my own life. I began to regard her as the example for all of us who wish to conceive and give birth to the Christ Spirit in our lives. This idea took on new meaning when I actually experienced what it may have been like to have been one of the maidens considered by God.

I had this experience for the first time during a baptismal service a few years ago. Although I had been baptized as a child, I felt that it was an appropriate thing to do it again—especially since it would be a full immersion.

The minister described the full immersion as an act of surrender. He advised me to lay myself down in the water and to surrender to the realization of my true spiritual identity.

When I entered the baptismal chamber, there were steps going down into a large pool area. When I saw those steps, something happened to me. I suddenly found myself with other young women on a flight of stairs—a place where I somehow knew God first designated Mary to be the channel of the Christ child. Needless to say, this vicarious experience has since become very, very important to me.

Subsequently, I "remembered" more about the experience, and recalled something else—my anger at God for not choosing me. *I wasn't mad at Mary, for she and I were friends in the experience:* I was mad at God. *I was angry because I couldn't see that Mary was any better than I was.* And then I realized I had fallen into the error of making comparisons between Mary and myself. *I realized, too, that as long as I was preoccupied with making such comparisons, I was not ready to become a channel for the Divine.*

Since then, meditation has brought Mary even closer to me. She has approached me many times in meditation. Sometimes she'll just appear and silently hand me a rose of one color or another. I know the particular colors have meaning, but I don't always know what to make of it.

As I was going into meditation one day, I asked of her, "How can I help to prepare the way for the return of Christ?" A little while later, she appeared to me in a vision and I saw her roll up her sleeves. It reminded me a little of what the nuns who taught me in grade school used to do: They would often fiddle with their robes when they were trying to get all that fabric out of the way. As Mary rolled up her sleeves, she took me by the hand and led me to a sink where we proceeded to wash dishes together. In that moment, we were just two women doing what needed to be done. *Interestingly, I have an expression that I have used before and since this encounter: "Talking doesn't do it, reading doesn't do it;* living is what does it." *And I always say that if you can't wash dishes with me, you haven't got it.*

Not long ago, I asked of Mary, "How can I be of greater use?" In apparent response to this question, she appeared to me in a clear vision. Instead of answering my question, she asked me, "Are you sure?" *It was as though she was asking if I really wanted to know the answer. Because she seemed so serious, I hesitated and did not give an immediate answer. So she repeated,* "Are you sure?" *And then I said "Yes," because I knew that I wanted to do my part.* (M.B.)

Common sense dictates that the process of serving God has nothing to do with a contest. If each of us has the capacity to enter into a state of profound spiritual responsiveness, then any one of us can serve God—if not as Mary did,[41] then surely in ways that spring from our own unique strengths. Of course, there are countless ways that the Spirit can use us in furthering the influence of love in this world.

Mary's question, *"Are you sure?"* reminds us that commitment itself may be more important than the particular direction we choose to take. She seems to say that there is no point in providing answers to our questions unless we are sure that we intend to follow through.

Regardless of the source of M.B.'s experience, her anguished "recollection" captures the psychological dilemma of virtually anyone who draws close to the Holy Family through the imaginary reliving of their experiences. The Catholic church has long supported such vicarious reenactments of the biblical drama—most notably through the *Spiritual Exercises of St. Ignatius of Loyola,* as well as through the fifteen mysteries of the rosary. These exercises involve visualizing and reliving the most significant moments in the unfoldment of Mary's and Jesus' lives.

What happens to us when we are willing to enter into these intense experiences? Inevitably, we begin to feel—as M.B. did— what Jesus and Mary may have felt, and to consider the ultimate questions that they once faced. Indeed, the more we vicariously retrace their steps, the more their willing sacrifices, in particular, bring into question our own capacity to do what they did, and to become what they became. How many of us have asked ourselves, for instance, Would I have consented to "let it be done unto me," knowing the disbelief that a virginal conception would have stirred? Or, could I, like Jesus, have shown such immense compassion in the face of the world's harsh treatment? Or, could I have witnessed my own son's crucifixion? It is only natural that we ask such ultimate questions of ourselves, for Jesus and Mary were humans, too, regardless of the lofty positions they have come to occupy in our tradition.

It is not surprising that most of us find it difficult to believe in our capacity to be like Mary and to welcome fully the coming of the Christ Spirit. Whether we feel overlooked as did M.B., most of us remain convinced that, ultimately, we are different from, and inferior to, Mary and Jesus.

Of course, we have had help in developing this pervasive and largely unexamined sense of inferiority. In the Judeo-Christian tradition—at least up until the time of Jesus—God remained forever separate and far off from us. He resided on the mountaintop, or in the Temple, but not within our hearts. Through Jesus, God presumably reached out and became one of us. But can we, in turn, build the bridge from our side of the great divide, and become as he is? Jesus seemed to say that we could and would—especially when he asserted that *we* were "gods" in the making, that *our* bodies were the temples of the living God, and that we would do greater things than even he did.

One time-honored tradition has been to imitate Jesus. However, because the orthodox position has emphasized Jesus' equivalence with God—and by contrast, our own sinfulness—Jesus looms much too large for most of us to think about imitating.

Because of this, imitating Mary has become an obvious substitute to the imitation of Christ. After all, she was one of us before and after she gave birth to the Christ. It is easier to imagine becoming what she was, f*or she assented to her calling from within the context of her humanness.* But, alas, Mary has drifted away from us, as well. As the church fathers asserted Jesus' prior and eternal oneness with God, Mary's humanness was similarly diminished, leaving her uniquely imbued with a kind of divinity by association. As Marina Warner points out, Mary's elevation to near-equal status with Christ has definitely had its downside.

Soaring above the men and women who pray to her, the Virgin conceived without sin underscores rather than allevi- ates pain and anxiety and accentuates the feeling of sinfulness. . . . Any symbol that exacerbates the pain runs counter to the central Christian doctrine that mankind was made and redeemed by God, and, more important, is a continuing enemy of hope and happiness.[42]

Two thousand years of theological speculation about Mary's greatness has ultimately rendered her much too far off and too fine to provide a ready example of how we might resolve our sense of separation from God. But as one Catholic priest recently remarked to a friend of mine, "People don't want theology; they want love." So, perhaps it is not surprising that many of us still venture to enter into an intimate, imitative relationship with this being in spite of the distance that organized religion has erected—however unintention- ally—between ourselves and her.

The process of imitating, and becoming like, the Blessed Mother has often begun with a surprising visit from her. Indeed, most of the recipients of the major historic apparitions were shocked when Mary first appeared to them. Even though Lucia of Fatima experienced earlier visions that can, in retrospect, be seen as preparations for the eventual apparitions, most of the visionaries had no foreknowledge that such blessings would ever come their way. In the following account, D.C. recounts her experiences of Mary's growing presence in her life. Like those individuals whom we have come to associate with Mary's major manifestations in our time, D.C. simply did not see it coming.

I had a difficult time growing up. When my father came back from the war, he became an alcoholic, so there were a lot of problems at home. Such experiences certainly send a person on a quest for meaning in life. At fifteen I was propelled forward to find God; so I decided then that I wanted to become a minister, but my father wouldn't let me. My religious background was Anglican, but now I am open to all religions.

When I was about twenty-one, and after our first son was born, I developed multiple sclerosis. For years, I felt that I would never get well. Late in my thirties, I went to a naturopathic doctor and improved somewhat. But in my forties I became very ill again—to the point where I felt I would never recover enough to carry on.

When I weighed about eighty-nine pounds, and was depleted and weak, I began desperately looking for healing in other ways. It was the beginning of a turnaround.

I had always been quite religious, but I hadn't visited psychics or spiritual healers. But during this time of desperation, I went to a woman who was a massage therapist and worked with healing prayer. After asking her to intercede for me, she received a message about a "Marie" who would facilitate my healing and the healing of others, as well. I was puzzled by the message, and at first I couldn't see how it related to my healing in any way.

Around 1989, I became very interested in facilitating the healing of others, even though I wasn't completely well myself. I became involved in various healing groups and began to pray for the intervention of the Holy Spirit. I still wasn't making any sense of the reference to a "Marie."

About this time, we asked a Catholic priest—Father Cox—to baptize my granddaughter. Thereafter, we went to him for counseling because we were having family problems.

At times, he and I talked alone about healing. When I was with him on one occasion, I began to see a blue flashing light filling the room. When I asked him if he was aware of it, he said, "Yes, and there seems to be more here today than usual."

As I knelt for him to bless my work with healing, I felt the energy cover my head. He said, "Of course, you know whose light this is, Dorothy."

I said, "No, I'm not quite sure." He said, "It's Mother Mary." I then thought "Marie! Mary! It's another name for Mother Mary!"

Since then, several of the people for whom I have prayed have experienced some tremendous changes. One woman, who had been praying every day for a month or more, asked me to assist her in the healing process. As I worked with her, she said she felt as though a curtain parted and a tremendous blue light came through to her. The energy was so powerful that she felt she was on fire. Somehow it brought healing to her. After the session was over she said, "I'm just burning up." Since we had both prayed to Mary, we attributed the healing energy to her.

Father Cox, who died recently, was very devoted to Mother Mary. One day I visited him, and again the room filled with such beautiful energy I thought I would levitate to the ceiling. I told him what was happening, and as he blessed me I felt a beautiful energy come over me. There was a storm that day, and as I walked home from church I thought, "How would we know for sure if we had been healed?" I asked this of the Holy Spirit.

That night I had the most remarkable dream. I was a child looking for the God of my childhood. As I walked up and down the streets looking for the Anglican sanctuary where I *had worshiped with my grandparents as a child, I came to a church that I recognized as the one I was looking for. I went in and entered the inner sanctum, which was filled with icons of Christ. Father Cox then came forward dressed in white.*

Then the door of the room opened, and a voice said, "I am the open door. No man cometh to me except through Christ." *Then Father Cox lifted me up, and the voice said,* "Thou art healed."

Following Father Cox's death, I went through a period of sadness, feeling that dying in his early forties was such a tragedy. I was sitting on the couch in my living room looking at baptisimal pictures of him with our children and feeling very sad, when suddenly Mary appeared before me in a flash of light. She was wearing a soft blue dress, and her light brown hair was covered with a white scarf.

She spoke to me in thought, saying, "He is where he is meant to be, doing what he is meant to be doing. Be at peace." *I was left with a feeling of peace and—in the days that followed—a sense of knowing there was a purpose to it all.*

That summer, my friend Helen told me about the events at nearby Marmora, a farm between Petersborough and Ottawa, Ontario, where Mary has appeared to thousands of visitors. Located in a tiny village, and owned by a family who has made many pilgrimages to Medjugorje, Marmora has a grotto and a healing spring. Helen told me that the Venezuelan visionary, Maria Esperanza de Biancini,[43] was coming to the farm and would talk about Mother Mary.

A few days later, four of us drove to Marmora for the first time to hear Maria Esperanza. I was quite moved by all the singing and the energy there. When I prayed, I didn't see the deep blue light that I usually see. Instead, I saw a rosy pink light everywhere.

The next day I was filled with energy and felt I had to write. I recognized that it was coming from Mary, so I prayed until the Holy Spirit was with me. I felt that she had a message for me because of my being in Marmora. I wrote the first message and was grateful that she was speaking to me. I wondered, "Will there be any more messages?" I received a "yes" for my answer.

About every second day I felt a surge of energy around my head and then resumed writing. When I asked how long it would last, I was told that there would be a total of twenty messages. I prayed every night. Whenever I felt the energy around me, I knew that it was time to write again.

We went back to Marmora on September 8—Mary's traditional birthday. It rained and then the sun came out. Sue and I knelt in the field and prayed. At one point, Sue nudged me and said, "Look up at the sun!" I thought, "Good heavens. I'm going to be blinded if I look at the sun." I tried to look up and saw it pulsing, but couldn't keep looking; so I closed my eyes and put my head down. Then I saw a rosy light, and out of this rosy light came Mary. She was dressed all in white, with a blue mantle over her head. Out of her heart came a flashing white light. Sue also saw her in the sun. We were ecstatic on the way home.

A few nights later in a dream I saw Mary as a white statue. I stood in front her, naked. I believe it meant that I could hide nothing from her. She knows our hearts and souls more than we do.

When I had the courage to put these messages into a booklet, I thought at first that they were meant just for me.

But I was told, "What would be for you would be for others, too."

Even though the messages seem simple, Mary says that she will give us more only once we have done the things that have already been given. In the messages, she tells us to go within to find our inner God-knowing. She urges us to live with our families in love each day, to say the rosary, and to have devotion to her, to Christ, and to God. Further, she wants us to thank God every day for the simple things.

The messages she has given me—such as the one that follows—are not so much prophetic messages, but simple messages about living our lives each day in communion with God.

Here I do come at this time to prepare the way for the coming of my son, Jesus. Just as John the Baptist foretold his coming to me, I come now to prepare you for him. I call to the lost sheep to come again into the fold of my mantle—to return to him through me. I call to you in love. At times I weep for the plight of my children and the many difficulties they are experiencing at this time. Here, now, is a time of purification, fasting, and reconciliation to my son through my immaculate heart. I call to all of my children to come to the remembrance of your oneness. For, as I look upon your faces, you are all mine. (D.C.)[44]

If we seek to imitate Mary and to incorporate her qualities of tenderness and responsiveness into our lives, we may eventually enter into a profoundly personal relationship with Christ himself. Or for persons like D.C. or myself, who were not raised in the Catholic church, a devotion to Jesus may eventually open our hearts to his mother, as well. In the following account, a woman comes to know Mary years after serving Jesus in remarkable ways. Her whole life revolves around the miraculous and the sacred, and serves as a faith-inspiring testimony of what can happen when we submit fully to a relationship with God.

I wasn't supposed to live when I was born, but my mother said the Lord told her to pray over me for I was special.

In my young life, I befriended children who were not liked. I was always helping people any way I could. For it seemed to be the thing I should do in my heart.

I met and married a young man from Illinois during the Second World War. I was born and raised around Rio Hondo, Texas, and was working in San Benito. After the war we moved to Illinois. My in-laws didn't like me, so I was alone with my daughter and I was pregnant with another child. But I knew Jesus as my personal Savior, and He and I had great conversations. He talked to my heart and taught me so much. He had me help people who were in need. There were times I'd be told to take food to a house, and the people there were always in need, and surprised that I had known about their problem. I shared Jesus with them and how he worked in my life.

When our fourth child, Kathy, was born, she had brain damage from the birth. The doctor and the nun in charge told me to pray for her to die. Jesus' words came out of my mouth, "She is a gift from the Lord." Jesus told me to lay hands on her head several times a day and she would be well. I did as he instructed and at seven months she finally responded to him. She was slow, but steady, as I prayed over her often.

When I went to the hospital to have our fifth child, Kathy was pulling herself up; she was twenty months old. I promised I would be back soon. After the baby came, I was hemorrhaging, and the head nun wouldn't let the doctor do a hysterectomy because I was only twenty-nine and Catholic, and had many more childbearing years. I overheard the doctor tell my husband I was going to die, as he couldn't do anything. I said, "Lord, I promised Kathy I would be home soon, so thanks for the healing." The blood flow stopped. Everyone was surprised, but I let them know it was a miracle from God. Soon I was home.

Our Kathy grew and by the time she was five, she went to kindergarten. She wore very strong glasses, but we continued the prayer and by the time she went to second grade, she wore no glasses. Today, she has three children of her own, teaches slow readers, maintains a prayer line, and is a very devoted Catholic.

I continued to help others, and tried to be the best mom and teacher.

In 1968 we won a trip to Portugal and Spain from my husband's company. On the way over on the plane, the Lord spoke to me and said I must go to Fatima. That was not in our plans, but I begged twenty-eight people to go with my husband and me, as we needed thirty to make the trip. We did go and while we were touring there, it began to rain. I ran into an open door, which turned out to be where the nuns from the hospital there came to pray. My husband and friends stayed outside, believing that we were not supposed to go in, but I was drawn to enter. I could hear soft music that was heavenly. I was compelled to kneel, and my head bowed down to the floor.

There were two nuns praying nearby. They never spoke, but at one point I heard a sound like the rustling of fabric. I looked up and there was the Blessed Mary. She was smiling at me and said, "Mary, you have found favor with my son

Jesus." *I stared at her for a minute, then I bowed my head down to the floor, and soon backed out of the room.*

I asked my husband and the two ladies who were with him if that wasn't the most heavenly music, and they said, "What music?" So I didn't tell them the Virgin Mary had appeared to me, for I was sure they would think I was crazy. She had also said for me to pray the rosary. I hadn't prayed the rosary very often, since I converted to Catholicism only when I married my husband.

Mary appeared to me again in our church on July 3, 1990. It was my deceased mother's birthday, and I asked God to give me a sign that my mom was with him. While Father Morris was saying the Mass, I looked up at Jesus on the cross behind the altar. Suddenly, Mary appeared at the priest's left side, holding her hand under his elbow. She smiled at me. I closed my eyes, opened them, and she was still there for another minute. I wrote Father Morris about it, and he said he felt a presence by him. He was sorry he didn't see her.

For the last twenty years I've taken patients to get chemotherapy and radiation treatments. I go into homes and pray with the sick. I have seen healings and made people realize how great it is to know the Lord personally.

I am a greeter, a lector, and a eucharistic minister at our church. I have a prayer line and I have a prayer meeting in my home, all prompted by the Lord. I am so blessed by being obedient to my Lord.

We have been married fifty-eight years, and have seven children who all know the Lord personally, thirteen grand-children, and one great-granddaughter. We come together as often as possible. I write to a lot of lonely people, and to my six grandchildren in college every week. (M.M.)

When we read M.M.'s account, we can feel her genuine humility and her profound love of God. More than just a moving story comes through: Her whole life has an infectious quality that can deepen our faith and motivate us to give ourselves more fully to God. These accounts are like precious fruit that take a lifetime to ripen, and the persons who share them are like trees among us to shelter us from doubt and loneliness.

Whether male or female, a lofty destiny is clearly intimated by the accounts that we have considered in this chapter: As we come to imitate the example that Mary provides us, we, too, will come to serve the Christ as his channels and companions in this world. C. S. Lewis captures this idea by saying that "what is above and beyond all things is so masculine that we are all feminine in relation to it." [45]

In the final analysis, we are called upon to become receptive and to submit to the Master's purpose and to his supremely affirming love. In the following two accounts, S.E. encounters God the Father, Jesus, and Mary, and communes with them in the Holy Light.

The reader should keep in mind that these two experiences actually represent the culmination of years of meditation and prayer work through which S.E. incrementally approached this fulfillment.

Early in 1989, I was meditating one day using what I call the "light prayer," and I found myself in a great hallway. It was ornately decorated and elegant like as castle. I was flying or floating down the hallway, passing pairs of angels posted on each side. They were very friendly and encouraged me onward. At the end of the hallway, I saw a double door, separated by a solid piece of wood. The angels opened the door on the right, and I entered.

I found myself in a great hall. It was empty except for three thrones, with three steps leading up to the thrones. Then I started flying from the doorway to the base of the three steps. I was surprised to see three persons seated: God the Father on my right, Christ in the middle, and Mother Mary on the left.

I was surprised to see what I considered to be a naive representation of God the Father. From my previous experience, I knew God as the Absolute, the Infinite, the Eternal, the Omnipresent source of all of creation. I had lots of direct experience of the magnificent transcendent God. So to have God sitting there in human form seemed quaint, and even naive, to me. But I had no control over this, and the vision continued.

I presented myself at the base of the steps and kneeled. I referred to him as my liege lord, and I was dressed as a knight without any armor. I swore my faithfulness and promised to do his will at all times.

The Father never looked directly at me. He wore jewel-encrusted slippers, with pants and robes made from heavily brocaded fabrics. His clothing was covered with gold, copper, and burnished colors. He wore a headdress that covered his head and blocked a view to his face.

I prostrated myself at his feet in adoration of him, but he reached down and lifted me and had me sit on his lap. I found great joy in discovering his fatherly affection toward me, but wondered why I could not see his face. Then, as he held me, he turned toward me and I could see him.

His face was pure light. *Beautiful golden white light.* He leaned in and kissed me with this light. I was absorbed into the light.

At that time, I don't think I was aware that the Bible says that you can't see the face of God and live. If I had read that, it wouldn't have mattered, because in my experience a *direct experience of God supercedes all jurisdictions. Perhaps you would die if you saw his face with earthly eyes, but not—I believe—with eyes of the Spirit.*

This experience recurred many times in meditation. Then, one day, he stood up, dropped his garment, and appeared before me as a shapeless figure of light. Then, my garment dropped away as well, and I was pure light, too. I moved toward him and merged with the light. I was still myself, but I was equally dispersed in his light.

Then Jesus and Mary stood up, shed their outer forms, and came into the light, as well. The four of us were as one. They showed me that this was our true nature, and that all of mankind is this light, and that all of sin can be erased by instantaneous forgiveness.

This was the most transforming experience I've had, and served as the basis for all that God has planned for me. This experience of my true nature comes back to me each day as I go through everyday circumstances.

A few months later, in August 1989, I returned to the throne room for a slightly different experience. This time, I encountered Jesus face-to-face.

I was in deep meditation and found myself in the same large, grand ballroom. Again, the room was empty except for steps leading up to three thrones. I was wearing the same gown I always do, except in my first visits to the throne room I was dressed differently. I was in a floor-length indigo blue velvet dress. I was barefoot, and my hair was long and loose (whereas in waking life, I have medium short hair).

I flew to the thrones without hesitating. On the right I saw the Father; in the middle, Jesus; and to my left, Mary. Jesus stood up and walked down the three steps. He was very handsome. He had long, medium-light brown hair, and wore a white, long-sleeved tunic. It reached his feet, which were bare.

I prostrated myself before him, but Jesus raised me up and escorted me a few steps forward. No words were spoken.

Then he turned to face me. He embraced me and leaned forward to kiss me. Just as our lips would have touched, everything abruptly changed. Instead of feeling his lips on mine, my consciousness expanded like a bomb exploding: Everything turned to light. It was wonderful. In that moment, I knew that he had married me and that our marriage would last forever.

After meditation, and for the next few days, approximately every twenty minutes I would feel intoxicated with the Holy Spirit. But it did not interfere with my daily chores. (S.E.)

S.E.'s experiences of spiritual union may represent the pinnacle experience of all of us who walk the spiritual path, yearning above all else for union with God. Through her experience, she has come to enjoy an extraordinary intimacy with the personhood of God. Some of us might find this uncomfortable. Thinking that God is somehow more austere and impersonal than our best friend, we might balk at the idea of embracing and kissing the Lord. Yet, the history of Christian mysticism reveals that communion with the Divine builds upon, rather than departs from, what we already know about love: It both resembles and overshadows our experience of human love.

In the end, S.E. exhibits a down-to-earth quality that rounds out her spiritual initiations: *Her chores still matter to her.* Like M.B., who learns from Mary that washing dishes serves God's unfolding purpose in this world, S.E. demonstrates an interest in what matters here and now. Like all genuine mystics, S.E. returns from the mountaintop, rolls up her sleeves, and embraces the work that lies before her. For her, that has meant supporting a Bosnian orphan, home-schooling two teenage daughters, and working in her own quiet way toward the unification of all Christian denominations.

Imitating Mary means becoming active in the world in a way that uplifts and heals others. Each of the above recipients has turned to some form of a healing ministry as a way of expressing their commitment to Mary and to God. It is clear from their accounts that our efforts are crucial in bringing about constructive change in the world, and that we must not simply await the Spirit's interventions in our lives. In essence, we can see that when we accept the invitation to imitate Mary, *we become that force of change that the world desperately needs.*

The following two accounts reveal the impact we can have on situations that are constantly unfolding in our lives. Both recipients have had multiple experiences with Mary and Jesus, and now serve them whenever called to do so.

I awakened in the middle of the night on Christmas Day in 1977 and felt guided to go to my altar and pray to Mary. I remained there for about half an hour in prayer when the phone rang at around 1 A.M. A friend was calling to ask me to pray for his wife who was in advanced labor. They were having a home birth and the midwife couldn't get there in time to deliver the baby, so the husband had to do the job. I went back to the altar to pray. White light filled the whole room and the presence of the Mother filled me with waves of powerfully intense but very serene energy as I focused prayers on the birth process. The energy waves subsided gradually as the experience came to a close. Then the phone rang and my friend elatedly announced the birth of his second daughter; the mother and child were both in good health. (C.N.)

My favorite place on earth to go when the burdens of the world became too much is the Grotto of Lourdes in Emmittsburg. Here I've had several occasions to hear Mary's voice.

Three years ago, I went to the Grotto to thank Mary for a healing. While in prayer, I saw the silhouette of a full-term pregnant woman. I asked Mary, "Who is it?"

She said, "Your daughter."

I asked, "Is she pregnant now or will she be?"

Mary answered, "Pray for the unborn child." Two months later my daughter announced she was pregnant. I continued to pray every morning and night. The baby was born nine weeks early. He could breathe on his own but only had an immature digestive system. Today, he is a healthy, happy, loving child. I feel Mary's vision and words to encourage me to pray saved his life. I have always had a great devotion to Mary and feel she guides my steps. (C.L.)

In the initial encounter with those who seek to imitate her, the Blessed Mother bestows her love and protection, but eventually, she calls us to action—to bring the Christ Spirit into fuller manifestation. Whether it is to rededicate ourselves to our marriages, engage in intense prayer for the redemption of mankind, or to engage in a healing work, a ministry of some kind awaits us as part of our "marriage" with the Christ Spirit.

And yet, the call to action is one that few of us feel ready to undertake. Indeed, we might protest that we are too weak, or too inexperienced, to serve God in any significant way. My former client, Rachel, voiced her own sense of unworthiness at the end of her great vision with Mary that began this book. As the reader may recall, Rachel awoke to see a star outside her window. As she marveled at its beauty, it grew into an orb of light, out of which Mary descended from the sky. As she took Rachel's hands, she said *"This is what you have been searching for."* And then, Mary proceeded to teach her a method of healing that she wanted her to teach to others. Let us now consider the rest of Rachel's encounter.

... "This is what you have been searching for."

I interpret her words to mean that I have been searching for a way to heal others through laying on of hands, which is true.[46] *Once again, I am flooded with tears.*

She then says, "Do it this way." And then she is in front of me and behind me and within me, too, guiding my every movement. Her arms wrap around me, and become my arms. I marvel that this can be so, but like a child, I just accept that it is happening. Throughout the vision, I have no feelings of unworthiness.

I am aware now that my dear ones are hovering very closely as if observing what Mary is teaching me. And you,[47] *dear one, you are in front of me and to my right; and you, too, are bathed in this beautiful light. I am not aware of the sound, for it seems that the sound has transported us to this place. Yet, I am in my bedroom, too, with my furniture glowing.*

My hands are moving to trace a spiral movement to the client's head and then stopping at the heart.

She again says, "Do it this way." And it is her voice and my voice at the same time.

"Right hand facing down, open palm," *she continues. And my hand lowers.*

Mary then says, "This was the stake used to crucify the Christ, called Jesus. Up with the hand, still facing down, then over to the right with the palm leading. Exhale to eliminate all fears. This also eliminates the cross from the stake. Now with both hands, gather up the spirits, all natives—especially those American Indians, black people, Jews, and all who have been persecuted in the name of religion, or by someone in their own family. Gather in this deep betrayal, this hurt that J.J. [my son] has said, 'You will never forget, Mama, it will never go away.'"

She goes on: "Draw this up with both hands—this was the three days that Jesus spent under the evil force—it was necessary. Draw this up with your arms and open hands and open loving heart—once again, through the stake on which Jesus was nailed. Join open hands, eliminating the original cross, stake, or sin. As your hands come together at the top of the stake, form a cup. You have found the Holy Grail. Hold this for a moment."

I am aware at this point that I am being held upright by Mary. I am sobbing completely. You, dear one, put your hand on my shoulder and say clearly but silently, "Everything will be all right."

She then says, "Hold this for a moment. Let the tears overflow. 'My cup runneth over.' Now, with both hands to the right, one supporting the other, visualize the pictures you have seen of the heart pierced by the sword. This is the sword that pierces so many hearts—mothers who have lost children and do not understand why. Like you, Rachel; like Mary, the mother of Jesus; like so many. Only a mother knows this pain—of giving birth and then watching that one die."

Then it dawns on me that she knows me as I am in my human form. Mary knows that you called me Rachel in your book; and she knows my son J.J., who has come close to death so many times; and she knows that I gave birth to little Joe who died.

She then forms my hands into a circle or a tunnel, and she moves it slightly to my left. Then, the shaft of light pours through it, along and over the sword. The light is only one color now—all blue, and it completely eliminates the sword. The light streams through the sword, and it is gone.

"This sword can now be transformed with the light. Bring your hands together over your heart to receive a blessing from me to you.

"You are united forevermore.

"Bow your head into your open hands. Reunion."

Mary then says, "Now, Rachel, sunny girl, go and teach. Go and teach. Everything will be all right. Do not doubt. This is all. . ."

She smiles so sweetly. But she immediately takes in my condition and my sense of desolation at being left alone, and she adds, ". . . for now!"

All my dear ones and you, dear one, move in to support me and console me as she moves up the shaft of light, taking it with her. At this point I have literally collapsed, and I am being supported by the dear ones, and you still have your hand on my shoulder.

As she withdraws, I protest that I cannot teach.

She says, "You can. There is only love."

She reaches down and takes my hands away from my heart and forms them into a cup in front of me. She knows that the distance is growing between us, and that I am devas-

*tated that I cannot follow. She smiles and says, "*From my heart into your hands, a touch of love. You have done well.*"*
    Blue light beams into my hands, and she is gone.

We are truly fortunate to have the testimonies of individuals like Rachel, who share a mystical relationship with Mary, and whose whole lives now revolve around imitating her example in their individual ways. *But we can do the same.* Even if we never encounter Mary face-to-face, we can still come to *feel* the Blessed Mother as an abiding inner presence, and to sense our own unfolding responsiveness to serve as channels of the Spirit. Through that inner work, we can come to know the feminine face of God, and imitate her example just as surely as those who have seen the colors of Mary's mantle and heard her quiet words quell the mind's incessant chatter.

And when we attempt to disqualify ourselves from the great work that God calls us to do, let us remember that he once asked the greatest of things from someone just like us—and that above all, *there is only love.*

Rosary Prayer

O God,
Whose only begotten Son,
by his life, death, and resurrection,
has purchased for us the rewards of eternal life,
grant we beseech Thee,
that meditating on these mysteries
of the most holy Rosary of the Blessed Virgin Mary,
we may imitate what they contain,
and obtain what they promise,
through the same Christ our Lord.
Amen.

Medjugorje

ON JUNE 24, 1981, SIX CHILDREN FROM MEDJUGORJE in Bosnia-Herzegovina—Ivanka Ivankovic, Mirjana Dragicevic, Vicka Ivankovic, Ivan Dragicevic, Ivan Ivankovic, and Milka Pavlovic—encountered a beautiful young woman on a hill called Podbrdo. The lady, who carried a child in her arms, said nothing, but beckoned for the children to come closer. The children were too afraid to approach her, even though they all believed that she was the Blessed Mother.

The next day, the children agreed to meet again in the same area. Two of the original six children—Ivan Ivankovic and Milka Pavlovic—were not present, but two others joined the group. From that day onward, Maria Pavlovic and Jakov Colo became a permanent part of the original group, while Ivan and Milka were never able to see the lady again, even though they tried.

On that second day, the children saw a flash of light, and then the lady appeared again, this time without the child. She was smiling and joyful, and indescribably beautiful. Again she gestured for them to come forward, which they did with some trepidation. They fell on their knees before her and began to pray the Our Father, Hail Mary, and Glory Be. She prayed with them, except during the Hail Mary. As she disappeared, she blessed them saying, *"God be with you, my angels!"*

On the third day, the children returned to the hillside again and saw three flashes of light just prior to seeing the lady appear. It was on this day that Mirjana asked the lady her name, to which she replied, *"I am the Blessed Virgin Mary."* By the fifth day, over 15,000 people accompanied the children to the apparition site. Vicka asked the lady what she wanted from the people and the priests. The lady summarized her intent in simple terms: *"The people should pray and firmly believe."* As for the priests, Mary said that they should believe firmly and help others to do the same.

The Blessed Mother has continued appearing to the six visionaries on a daily basis at 5:40 P.M. Medjugorje time. In addition to issuing messages about the things that we can do to make a difference in the world, Mary has outlined a sequence of events that will unfold prior to the occurrence of a great chastisement. Reminiscent of Garabandal, the Blessed Mother originally stated that this terrible event would occur only if we did not do what was needed to avert the consequences of our past sinfulness. More recently, however, Mary has told the visionaries that the chastisement will necessarily take place, for it is apparently too late to avert it completely.

The full details of the chastisement, and the events that will precede it, have been imparted to the seers as ten secrets. Mary made it clear from the beginning that once a seer has received the tenth secret, she would cease appearing to them on a daily basis.

Mirjana was the first to receive the full complement of secrets on Christmas Day in 1982, and she now sees the Blessed Mother once a year on her birthday, and on the second day of each month. Two of the others—Jakov and Ivanka—have also received the tenth secret, and now see Mary only once a year.

The visionaries tell us that once they have all received the ten secrets, the apparitions will cease altogether, and the events prophesied will commence. In the meantime, the Blessed Mother continues to call all of us to engage in peace, faith, conversion, prayer, and fasting. In terms of specific practices, she has laid out what she calls the "five stones," or weapons, that will defeat the influence of Satan in the world: prayer, fasting, reading the Bible, confession, and the partaking of the Eucharist.

Like Garabandal, the commissions that have been appointed by the local bishop have failed, as yet, to confirm the supernaturality of the Medjugorje apparitions. Most would agree that the problem lies not so much in the veracity of the apparition, but in the unsettled relations between the bishops and the Franciscan parish priests that go back hundreds of years. Thus far, the bishops have issued a neutral statement, neither approving of the apparition, nor restricting the faithful from visiting the site: "We bishops, after a three-year-long commission study, accept Medjugorje as a holy place, as a shrine. This means that we have nothing against it if someone venerates the Mother of God in a manner also in agreement with the teaching and belief of the Church. . . . Therefore, we are leaving that to further study. The Church does not hurry" (*Glas Koncila,* August 15, 1993).

In respect for the authority of the local bishops, the Holy See has refrained from taking a position on the matter. However, it is well known that Pope John Paul II has affirmed on many occasions his heartfelt respect for the Medjugorje apparition. In a private conversation with the visionary Mirjana in 1987, the pope said, "If I were not pope, I would already be in Medjugorje confessing."

7

RESPONDING TO
Mary's Request

"Do whatever he tells you." (John 2:5)
Mary's words at the wedding at Cana

AS WE OPEN OUR MINDS AND HEARTS TO MARY, WE
begin to realize that she comes to convey a simple request. Whether
she remains silent and invites the recipient to *feel* what she wishes,
or conveys her message in simple terms for a visionary to share with
others, her intention never wavers: *She wants us to submit fully to a
relationship with God.* Indeed, when Lucia, the principal visionary
at Fatima, was asked to summarize Mary's most important message
at Fatima, she said, "The main request of our Lady is that we offer
up each day whatever God requests of us." [48]

Mary's own life demonstrates this process better than anyone
else's in our tradition. Just as Jesus represents the culmination of

the process of God becoming incarnate, Mary represents the consenting partner who sees the process through to completion.

Not surprisingly, Mary's manifestations to individuals reveal various steps that we can take toward embracing her spirit of consent and "offering up" whatever God asks of us. As a final stage in our examination of Mary's manifestations, I have summarized some of the steps that we can take toward fulfilling her "simple" request.

We Can Commune with Mary

It is clear from all of the testimonies that we have considered that the Blessed Mother calls upon each of us to accept the *direct* experience of her presence as a first step toward responding to our spiritual calling more fully than ever before. She does not expect any of us to remain on the outside looking in. She invites us to come under the protection of her mantle, and to find a relationship with her that is deeply fulfilling and secure. In traditional Catholic terms, the wearing of the scapular announces our willingness to come under the mantle of her love, once and for always. Whether we are Catholic or not, the scapular symbolizes something precious to which most of us can relate—*a loving relationship that will never fail us.*

The brown scapular traces its origins to a vision of Mary in 1241. On returning to England from the Crusades, Saint Simon Stock—the head of the Carmelite order—experienced a vision of Mary now well known to Roman Catholics. Since the Carmelites were under pressure from the more established orders in England at the time, its leader appealed to the Blessed Mother for assistance. In his vision, Mary told Simon that anyone who died wearing the brown robe of the Carmelites would be granted immunity from eternal fire. Mary's pronouncement had the effect of making the wearing of a small piece of brown wool—symbolic of the Carmelite robe—popular among the laity. Since then, countless people have worn the brown scapular as a visible sign of the Blessed Mother's love and protection.

To enjoy a perpetual sense of communion with the Blessed Mother, we must be willing to *submit* to her protection. To put it simply, *we must become like her children.* This is where many of us part company with Mary and Jesus and the personhood of God, for such a leap of faith often bears an uncomfortable resemblance to earlier experiences in which other protectors may have failed us and in which our trust gave way to disillusionment.

One man, who was abused as a child, recalls that the Blessed Mother came to him when he was nine years old to offer him the love and security that his parents could not give him.

It first happened when I was nine years old. I grew up in a very abusive family. Verbally and physically, I seemed to have become the punching bag for my parents. Around that time, I remember thinking that the best thing for me would be to die.

One night, while I was listening to my parents fighting, I fell asleep for what seemed to be only a second. When I awakened, I saw a woman who seemed to shine or radiate, but most of all I felt love and understanding pouring out from her to me. She took my hand and asked me to come with her—not verbally, but mentally. As soon as I touched her hand, I found myself high above the earth, and it was unbelievably beautiful. She told me that life was worth living, and at that moment I seemed to understand the real meaning of life, and why we're all here. Not a word was spoken, but there was a very sacred feeling.

I remember I could have traveled to the farthest planets with her, but I said that I'd better get home. Ever since that time, life has become easier and more rewarding for me.

The woman appeared to me again in my bedroom two months after my father died. She smiled at me and then disappeared, leaving the room smelling like flowers. Once again, I understood why we are here. (D.B.)

From the outside, it may seem as if D.B. can rest hereafter in the protective embrace of the Blessed Mother's love. But those of us who need love the most may have the most difficult time accepting it. For, having known abuse and betrayal early in life, it is no simple matter to turn our lives over to anyone, even God.

Ultimately, perhaps, we all bear some wounds from childhood that keep us from receiving God's love without recalling past wounds. So, not surprisingly, our first attempts to come under Mary's protection can bring us face-to-face with this unfinished business.

As we face the challenge of healing our memories from childhood, we might ask ourselves, *What do I need to do to resolve any leftover feelings of mistrust and betrayal that could get in the way of submitting more fully to a relationship with the Divine?*

We Can Engage in Regular Spiritual Practice

Beginning with the European apparitions in the 1840s, Mary has urged us to engage in daily spiritual practice. In particular, she recommends the recitation of the rosary, a practice that is still foreign to most non-Catholics. In several of the apparitions, the visionaries have observed Mary wearing the rosary beads on her wrist. Beginning with Bernadette's encounter with Mary at

Lourdes, the visionaries have recited the rosary along with Mary during some stage of the apparition's unfoldment. And, in many of the personal visions that we have considered, Mary wears the rosary 'or offers it to the recipient to be used in their spiritual practice. As the reader may recall, Mary offered her rosary to C.H. to be kissed at a time in his life when his commitment was wavering (see Chapter Four). Of all the features associated with Mary's appearances, the rosary is the most prominent symbol of the spiritual practice she wants us to do.

According to legend, Mary appeared to Saint Dominic[49] in the early 1200s and gave him the first rosary, saying, "This is the precious gift that I leave to you." However, the rosary evolved into its present form over the course of many centuries. The prayer that is repeated most often in the recitation of the rosary, the Hail Mary, is a synthesis of three separate sentences. The first two statements are taken from two New Testament passages—the angel Gabriel's salutation to Mary (Luke 1:28) and Elizabeth's greeting to Mary (Luke 1:42). This part of the Hail Mary was used as early as the fourth century. The last sentence, "prompted by a need to join petition with praise,"[50] was introduced in the seventh century. The word *Jesus* was added in the 1300s. Finally, the current version was formally adopted in the sixteenth century. It is as follows:

Hail Mary, full of grace, the Lord is with you. Blessed are you among women, and blessed is the fruit of your womb, Jesus. Holy Mary, Mother of God, pray for us sinners, now and at the hour of our death. Amen.

Obviously, the recitation of the rosary represents an evolving form of spiritual practice. Thus, it is understandable that many individuals have felt inspired to modify its prayers somewhat according to their particular needs and preferences. This seems to be in keeping with what the Blessed Mother wants of us—a heartfelt devotion rather than a mere repetition of words. In support of this view, Conchita of Garabandal said that Mary never cited the advantages of particular prayers when she spoke of the importance of reciting the rosary: It was the practice itself that was most important. Father Pelletier believes that when Mary emphasized the *practice* over the selection of the prayers, she was "attempting to reach the broadest possible number of souls and therefore did not want to propose a form of prayer that would definitely go beyond the reach of some and that could easily discourage many others." [51]

Beyond advocating the disciplined recitation of the rosary, Mary also emphasized *how* one should recite the rosary—that is, with deep feeling and careful concentration. To this end, she recommended praying *slowly* with emphasis on each word, and pausing between phrases. Onlookers who overheard Conchita and the other three girls praying the rosary along with the apparition were impressed with their slow, careful enunciation of each word. By having them pray in this way, Mary assisted the girls in recapturing the meaning of the prayers so easily lost in the hasty repetition of familiar words.

We might ask ourselves, *What form of spiritual practice am I called upon to do? Do I need to accept Mary's gift of the rosary, or venture into other forms of devotional practice?*

We Can Take Bold Steps to Change Our Lives

From the evidence that these accounts provide, it should be clear to us by now that Mary sometimes intervenes to steer us in bold new directions. She comes not only to invite us into her protective embrace and to engage us in spiritual practice, but also to illumine our individual and collective denial of what we are doing that can, in time, precipitate disastrous consequences.

In many of the major apparitions, Mary indicates that we must work diligently to atone for our collective choices if we wish to avert an eventual worldwide chastisement. Fortunately, Mary brings us the good news, as well—that individual prayer and meditation, and other "microcosmic" gestures of love, can exert a powerful impact on our collective fate. A few of us can apparently make all the difference in the world.

As a psychotherapist working on the level of the individual psyche, I have also come to realize that we each face our own individual "chastisements," if you will, if we remain in denial about the need to make significant changes in our current relationships, careers, and personal behaviors. Of the many personal encounters with Jesus and Mary that I have studied, many of them mention, or at least bring to mind, unresolved *personal* issues that stand in the way of a closer relationship with the Divine and our fellow human beings. A few of them even call for immediate action in order to avert tragic personal consequences. Like the Holy Family who was warned by the angel to flee Herod's soldiers, we, too, may need to take firm and dramatic steps to protect what is most precious to us from the consequences of our own choices—or from the destructive intentions of others. My first encounter with Christ in the early 1970s, for example, made it clear to me that I had to take bold steps if I wanted to remain on this earth.

I dreamed that I was actually flying around inside a new building with a friend. It seemed we were involved in praying for, or consecrating, the building. At one point, I saw my friend standing in a doorway at the back of the auditorium, talking to someone standing beyond the threshold. I knew it was Jesus! Knowing then that I was dreaming, I anxiously walked toward the door, hoping he would still be there. I passed through the door and looked toward where I assumed he would be. At first I was only able to see bright white light. But then I could see a man clearly in the midst of the light. He was strikingly handsome.

I stood silent and awed by his presence. I felt great love from him, but sternness, as well. He finally asked me, "Are you ready to leave the earth yet?" *I realized that he was asking if I was ready to die. Startled by the implications of his question, I said, "No."* He then said, "Then go out and do what you know to do."

Rarely does a day go by that I don't ask, *Am I doing what I know to do?* Indeed, this question is never "out of date."

As sobering as these encounters may seem at first, they may wake us up before it is too late, and keep us from straying from our true course. After mustering as much honesty that we can, we might ask ourselves, *What bold steps must I take in my life to remain true to my spiritual calling?*

We Can Accept That We Are Worthy of Love

When an encounter with Christ or the Blessed Mother is imminent, many of us abort the experience, because we fall prey to the erroneous belief that we are not worthy to receive them. One woman, for instance, dreamed that Jesus came knocking on her door. Believing that her house was too messy, she refused to open the door. Like this woman, most of us keep God waiting because we think we have to "clean up our act" first.

In contrast, most encounters with Mary and Jesus alike leave recipients convinced, regardless of whatever else might be true, that they are loved and that they are worthy. The reader may recall that one woman heard Mary say, *"I choose you,"* and another heard her say, *"I'm just like you."* These affectionate, inclusive messages are by no means extraordinary. Indeed, most of the spoken messages in the visions that have been included in the previous chapters reiterate this basic assurance that she loves us without condition.

Our sense of unworthiness is often rooted in our unwillingness to embrace the basic human impulses that seem so disruptive to our spiritual lives. In striving for spiritual purity, many of us have suppressed our sexual and aggressive urges under a facade of outward spirituality. Not long ago, I had a dream in which I discovered with some horror that I, too, may have "killed" the natural man within me.

The first part of the dream concerns my discovery of a great tragedy—the murder of a native American man by a group of white hunters who considered the Indian as no more than just another animal to be hunted. I am so deeply saddened and outraged as I discover this crime that I know I have to report it to the authorities.

After calling and reporting this tragedy, I feel at peace, like I've done something that will make a real difference.

Suddenly, I realize that this is all a dream. At first, I walk slowly across a grassy area, carefully observing the beauty of everything around me in the dream. A large hibiscus towers over me, and its dewy red blossoms droop down over my head.

From the memory of past lucid dreams, I know that the divine light is probably close at hand. So I raise my eyes to look for it above me, and I see an orb of white light filling the southern sky. I know that the light is Christ's light. A halo of light—like feathery lace or delicate latticework—radiates outward from it.

Then I notice an elderly woman approaching from behind me. I feel great love from her, so I greet her by putting my arm around her and kissing her on the forehead. I know somehow that she is the Blessed Mother.

We stand together and look up at the light, and see that there is a second light to our left and slightly below the white light of Christ. The second light resembles a maypop, or passion flower blossom, with bluish and lavender hairlike petals radiating outward from a white cross.

I turn to her and ask, "Is that your light?"

She nods.

I look back and see that there is now a third light—to our right and, again, slightly below the light of Christ. It is also bluish purple, and it shines from an open window on the top of a tower that has spiral steps leading upward.

I ask Mary, "Whose light is that?"

She says, "It's Mary Magdalene's light."

"Do you want to go there?" I ask her.

She nods again.

So we begin climbing the steps of the tower. Then I awaken.

My sense of horror over the murdered Indian reflected my growing awareness that I had abandoned the natural self in my lifelong attempt to become more spiritual, and that it was time to embrace my humanness if I was to rise to my fullest potential in serving God. Seeing Mary Magdalene's light beside Christ's light underscored the importance of our humanness on the spiritual journey. For regardless of who Mary Magdalene really was, tradition identifies her as the prostitute that Jesus rescued from stoning, as well as the first witness to the Resurrection. She was regarded by the early church as a peerless follower of Jesus, and became known as the first disciple, which means "witness." All of this suggests that no matter how "fallen" we may seem to be, we have an honored place beside him. Indeed, when the Blessed Mother accompanies me up the steps, she silently celebrates Mary Magdalene's humanity—and by implication, her own and mine, as well.

The Blessed Mother did for me what she has done for countless seekers: She left me knowing that the ageless dream of our suitability as partners to God is one that will eventually come true—once we can approach him free of a sense of our unworthiness.

If we are committed to a path of imitating Mary and conceiving the Christ Spirit in our own lives, then obviously we must hold fast to the conviction that we are worthy of the task. We might then ask ourselves, *Do I consider myself unworthy of God's love? Have I rejected an essential part of myself that I need to reclaim?*

We Can Accept the Price of Being in the World

No matter how much we are blessed with experiences of divine presence—whether it comes in the form or Mary, Jesus, an angel, or the less personified presence of the Holy Spirit—the stress of life can erode our sense of meaning and undermine our commitment to the spiritual path. Our infrequent moments of spiritual communion can seem irrelevant, at best, when compared to the real-life pressures that bear down upon us. In the following encounter with Mary, the recipient, S.E., whose other accounts were considered in the previous chapter, receives a simple but profound teaching applicable to us all.

I was in my bedroom making the bed. I stopped abruptly because I instantly knew, with great excitement, that Mary was coming tonight. That's all I knew, and I continued making the bed. After a full day of normal activity, I went to bed without thinking about the "announcement" I had felt earlier in the day.

Later, while asleep, I became lucid—that is, aware that I was dreaming. I was being escorted down a hallway of an elegant building by two men in suits. They walked beside me, each of them holding my arm, guiding me along.

We passed by an open door on my left. It was a small cluttered room. I glanced in and I saw a statue about two and a half feet tall of the Blessed Mother. It was made of gray stone. The statue was tilted, carelessly laid among the "stuff." As soon as I saw the statue, I lost all my composure and screamed in desperation, "Mother! Please come to me." I surprised myself with the intensity of my need for her.

At that moment, the two men held me more firmly and led me past the door to an elegant bench that was set against the wall of the hallway. They left me there. As I sat waiting, I looked toward the doorway to the room.

All of a sudden, a bare foot stepped through the doorway, followed by a glowing pink skirt. It was Mary! She walked out of the room, looking tall, strong, and very real. She was truly glowing. Every inch of her was glorified. She was wearing a pink dress, topped with a baby blue cape with a hood.

She walked over to the bench and sat down beside me. I was stunned and said to myself, "This is an apparition." I relaxed and opened myself to absorb her presence. She sat close to me and leaned in to speak to me. I looked into her eyes and found I couldn't look anywhere else. There was a magnetic force—a force that held my eyes. I said to myself, "This is why people say she is so beautiful; it's the magnetism."

She was beautiful, but she did not look like the statue. I can only say that her eyes were all black. She talked and she talked. I never said one word. She told me many things, but I was only able to remember one message. She told me that when bad things happen, there was something that I could do. At this point, even though I looked into her eyes, I had a vision of the little statue in the room. As I saw it from a close-up position, I noticed little dust balls hanging from her chin. The statue was dusty all over.

She said, "The dust that was thrown on my life was from the devil." *(I understood the dust to mean the distractions, inconveniences, and malicious behaviors.)*

She then said, "Wipe the dust away and I am there."

When I woke up the next morning, I felt great. In the days that followed, whenever I felt stress, I would remember her words and feel her knees and see her leaning in, speaking so intimately to me. She has always *been there.* (S.E.)

S.E.'s encounter reminds each of us that we face a simple choice in every moment—whether to succumb to the temptation of hopelessness and victimization, or to make the effort to find God's abiding presence beneath the dust that so often enshrouds our lives. The message assures us of Mary's immanence, but it also reminds us of the work we must do to claim what is available to us.

Another woman, who was ill and feeling lost, had a simple dream that assured her of God's presence in her life in spite of how she felt at the time.

Last spring, I came down with a nasty bout of flu from which I became very ill and feverish. I dreamt that I was lost and searching for something. I came upon a statue of Mary holding the infant Jesus. In that moment, I felt that she was reassuring me that she and Jesus are with me always, even when I feel lost. I awoke the next morning feeling better. It seems that Mary comes at those times in my life when I feel lost and I'm searching for meaning and reassurance that I'm on the right path.

When I feel overwhelmed and lost, I only have to look out my window to see an unusually large and thorny rose bush covered from late spring to fall in a mass of red blossoms. It reminds me that the rose that Mary was—and that we are, too—can coexist gracefully with the thorns of life. (D.C.)

We might then ask, *How can I learn to trust the loving presence that is always there—beneath the dust and amid the thorns of my life?*

We Can Restore a Sense of Harmony in a Fragmented World

We live in a time of psychological, social, and biological threat—when the structures that once held us together have weakened under the influence of cynicism, selfishness, terrorism, and more virulent forms of disease. This erosion of integrity is evident on all levels, and we desperately need something that will reestablish our sense of security and wholeness.

When my mother was diagnosed with pancreatic cancer and given a few months to live, I felt the tremors of emotional and familial disintegration. I turned to prayer as a way to help her and myself at the same time. Before I got down to concerted prayer, I spent several days painting a mandala—a healing ritual I discovered by accident when I was an adolescent and have repeated periodically ever since. *Mandala* is a Sanskrit word that means "circle." It defines any circular, square, or otherwise radially symmetrical design, usually based on the number four, or multiples of four. Mandalas have traditionally been associated with wholeness and healing. According to Jung, who studied mandalas extensively in his psychological studies, "the mandala is based on the premonition of a center of personality, a kind of central point within . . . to which everything is related, by which everything is arranged, and which is itself a source of energy." [52] Mandala forms can be found in all sacred traditions, including Christianity, where the cross, the rose, and the heart are important symbols for evoking a sense of the sacred.

I often painted mandalas spontaneously when I was young, during times of stress and upheaval. Looking back, this was not surprising, for the mandala—like a good mother—encircles and contains us during times of crisis. So, as the consuming force of cancer threatened my mother's health—and, in turn, my own emotional equilibrium—I used the mandala to draw upon an ever-available motherly force of spiritual protection and containment for both of us.

After completing the mandala, I meditated on the image and prayed for her well-being. I cannot say for sure if my prayers had anything to do with her recovery, but she went into remission for almost three years before she abruptly died. I have been told that only about one person in a hundred lives that long with pancreatic cancer. My stepbrother, who is a very down-to-earth physician, said to my brother and me after she died, "It does *not* happen that way. Her recovery had little to do with the chemotherapy. Something miraculous kept the cancer at bay, and that 'something' ceased to function all at once, right before she died." Whatever we call it— whether Christ, Blessed Mother, or Holy Spirit—it encircled the threat within my mother's body and restored her health for a season.

This all happened before I had accepted a relationship with the Blessed Mother. I was moving in that direction, but I had not arrived at the point where I could call her by name and accept the comforting presence that awaited me. But I was coming to know her in less personified forms. In one exquisite dream, I encountered the Mother's love in the form of a three-dimensional mandala—a tiny gazebo that housed an awesome light.

In the dream, I was meditating and saw a flash of light. I got up and began to look for its source. I came to a garden, and saw a light shining in the middle of the garden. As I got closer, I could see that the light was coming from a large egg-shaped crystal object that was floating above the ground and was protected by a blue canopy. The whole arrangement looked like a tiny gazebo with the light in the center. The closer I got to the light, the brighter and more intense it became, and I felt deeply loved by it. *I knew that the light loved me completely and unconditionally as a mother might love a child, and that it was responding to the quality of love within my heart.* I walked away from the light and then returned to it. Once again, the closer I got, the brighter the light shone, and again I could feel a powerful love emanating from it. Then I walked down a path with an unknown woman beside me. A dove flew up and landed on my shoulder. I knew that the dove was also responding to the quality of love within my heart, and that its fearless attention was a great confirmation. Then I looked up ahead and saw the Master of the garden. He looked at me without speaking, awaiting our approach.

My experiences with the encircling images of the mandala and the gazebo bring to mind the reason that so many of us are drawn to the Blessed Mother at this time. Previously, the binding influences in society, in the church, in our families, and within our own bodies seemed adequate to counteract the influences that threaten those things of greatest value to us. But things seem to have changed.

In these times, we all need something strong enough to counteract the influences that threaten to undermine what is good and healthy. The containment that we need for our health and development is seriously threatened. The AIDS epidemic is one concrete example of our collective inability *on a bodily level* to withstand the forces of disintegration in the world. And the rise of terrorism points to the same inability *on a social and political level* to maintain a basic sense of civility upon which we all depend.

Some people advocate a return to "family values" as a way to reclaim the stability that we desparately need. Others extol the virtues of holistic treatment in boosting our immune system's response to new and more virile strains of disease. Of course, these are important remedies in today's unstable world. But it is also likely that the solutions go beyond anything that we can orchestrate on our own. We must commit ourselves to constructive action, yes, but we also need help—not from ordinary sources, but from *within and beyond ourselves* to restore our sense of integrity. In this context, the Blessed Mother offers us a way of containing the forces that would otherwise divide us. How? By committing ourselves to various forms of self-sacrifice—such as prayer, fasting, and repentance. *It may seem ironic, but Mary offers us containment and spiritual protection at the price of letting go of ourselves and by doing what God asks of us.*

No wonder she comes to us now, when we are most in need of a sacred enclosure to encircle the fragments of our former selves and to forge them into a new being conceived in love. Perhaps our need will motivate us to do what we have been loathe to do before— to surrender fully to God's will. The force of love that she brings to us, the tangible gifts that she bestows on us, and the acts of sacrifice that she requires of us, may work together to restore our capacity to contain and nurture the good within us and in the world.

We Can Serve the One Mary Serves

When Jesus was dying on the cross, he addressed his mother and his disciple John, who were keeping vigil nearby. He said something that people have wondered about since the beginning of Christianity: He referred to John as Mary's son, and to Mary as John's mother.

> *When Jesus saw his mother and the disciple whom he loved standing beside her, he said to his mother, "Woman, here is your son." Then he said to the disciple, "Here is your mother." And from that hour the disciple took her into his own home* (John 19:26–27).

On the surface, Jesus seems to have been saying, "Take care of each other now that I am leaving you." But one can interpret his words more globally as a final directive meant for us all. From this perspective, Jesus gave *us* to his mother and gave his mother to *us*. After surrounding himself with twelve men during his brief ministry—some of whom misunderstood him regularly, and one of whom betrayed him fatally—Jesus points us to his mother at the very end. Such a gesture raises a question that he himself never really addressed: Where *does* the feminine fit in our spiritual lives?

In the early 1200s, a powerful new myth arose that offered us something of an answer to this enigmatic question.

The story concerned the search for the Holy Grail, the chalice from which Jesus served his disciples at the Last Supper. Many storytellers contributed to its emergence, tracing the bold design of an emerging new vision of wholeness from pieces of earlier myths and stories. Like all great myths and spiritual truths, there are many versions, and the picture is never completely clear. We can comprehend such mysteries best by allowing ourselves to suspend our analysis and to *feel* their meaning.

Consumed with the idea that the lost Grail could be found if one were pure enough in heart, the legendary Grail knights went off in search of the Grail in every conceivable place. While the story revolves around the search for the Grail, the culmination of the myth goes beyond its mere discovery. It concerns the resolution of a longstanding problem—the wound of Amfortas.

Years earlier, a young prince by the name of Amfortas had been out looking for an opportunity to test his skills in battle, and he had become hungry. Searching for something to eat, he stumbled into the camp of a pagan knight where a fish was cooking over an open fire. Since no one was there, Amfortas set about to eat someone else's dinner. In some accounts, the fish was so hot that a piece fell upon him, and burned him so badly that it would not heal; but in other accounts, the pagan knight discovered the intruder, and began to fight him. According to this version, the knight wounded the prince with a lance before Amfortas could kill him. Thereafter, Amfortas languished in the Grail Castle, unable to heal of his wound.

The young Amfortas bears a resemblance to the disciple Peter, who cut off the Roman soldier's ear when Jesus was arrested, to Judas who betrayed Jesus, and to any number of impetuous males who have made a complete mess of things. Amfortas symbolizes that part of our nature—usually referred to as masculine—that zealously reacts without regard for what is required of us. All kinds of problems arise when we hastily try to claim the prize without regard to the various authorities, both pagan and holy, who might have something to say about it.

Then along comes Parsifal. We are told that in his youth, Parsifal stumbled into the Grail Castle, and witnessed an exquisite vision of the Grail. As the chalice appeared to him from behind curtains and floated past him, he sat speechless, overcome by its beauty. He didn't realize it, but he had failed a crucial test: He had failed to ask the question, Whom does the Grail serve? When he woke up the next day, the castle and the Grail had disappeared without a trace.

Little did Parsifal know, experiencing the Grail was not the end-point of his search. He had to rouse himself from silence, and to rise above the self-gratifying impulse that had blinded Amfortas in his quest for more basic sustenance. Like Mary, he had to consent to serve what the Grail served rather than simply partake of it. And in doing so, he would become the Grail, a vessel of the living Christ. If he had done this, the Fisher King's wound—borne of a similar error—would have been healed once and for all.

Years later, after many hard lessons, Parsifal found his way back to the Grail Castle. As a mature and seasoned knight, he again beheld the beauty of the Grail. This time, however, his voice served him well. Stirring himself out of the ecstasy of merely experiencing the Grail, he asked, *"Whom does the Grail serve?"* In asking this crucial question, Parsifal ceased to be the passive witness or the aggressive warrior: Like Mary, *he consented to become a vessel of the living Spirit.*

When I recall Parsifal's quest for the Holy Grail, I am reminded of my own spiritual journey. When the Holy Spirit first came to me as a young man, it awakened a love and a light so intense I could hardly bear it. Like Amfortas and Parsifal, I hungrily sought it again and again, mistakenly thinking that the experience of God's presence would fulfill my spiritual calling.

I did not see at first into the heart of the matter—that we are called to *serve the Spirit,* not only to experience it. Like Amfortas, we may attempt to possess it; or like Parsifal, we may remain unresponsive in a state of self-satisfied bliss. That is why, I believe, Jesus points us to Mary at the end of his life. He knows that we can quickly reach the limits of our own development. Without understanding and *feeling* Mary's surrender to *her* call, we cannot begin to answer *our own.*

Jesus himself brought this truth home to me in my last encounter with him, several years ago. He appeared in a dream and left me knowing without a doubt that loving Mary was the next step in my spiritual journey.

I dreamt that I was working on a writing project. An unknown man and woman stood quietly behind me as I typed on my computer. Suddenly, the monitor opened up like a curtain, revealing Jesus from the chest up, only a few feet away. He was bathed in a purple light. Needless to say, I was stunned.

> *He said,* "Do you love me?"
> *I said,* "Yes."
> *Then he asked,* "Do we love Mary?"
> *Puzzled by his question, I paused and said,* "Yes."
> *Then he said,* "Then you are my father and my brother."

Jesus' enigmatic words seem to weave together several scriptural passages[53] into a promise of what awaits us if we will simply accept his mother as our own.

The Blessed Mother's complete responsiveness to God is an ideal that few of us will ever fully emulate: All we can do is to try our best. Like Jesus' two radically simple commandments, Mary's singular appeal to us leaves little room for analysis and argument. It all comes to down to a question. *Will you do what God asks of you?*

It is my sincere hope that you and I can say, as Mary once did, *"Let it be with me according to your word"*—that we can offer ourselves to the one she serves, and fearlessly do whatever he requests of us.

In this way, I believe that we will finally become what we are destined to be—brothers and sisters of Christ, capable of fostering his Spirit in this world.

Magnificat

My soul magnifies the Lord,
    and my spirit rejoices in God my Savior,
for he has looked with favor on the lowliness of his servant.
    Surely, from now on all generations will call me blessed;
for the Mighty One has done great things for me,
    and holy is his name.
His mercy is for those who fear him
    from generation to generation.
He has shown strength with his arm;
    he has scattered the proud in the thoughts of their hearts.
He has brought down the powerful from their thrones,
    and lifted up the lowly;
He has filled the hungry with good things,
    and sent the rich away empty.
He has helped his servant Israel,
    in remembrance of his mercy,
according to the promise he made to our ancestors,
    to Abraham and to his descendants forever."
(Luke 1:46–55)

Footnotes

1 G.S. Sparrow, *Blessed Among Women: Encounters with Mary and Her Message* (New York: Harmony, 1997).

2 Rachel was suffering from severe jaw pain at the time.

3 The rest of Rachel's magnificent vision is included in Chapter Six.

4 J. T. Connell, *Meetings with Mary—Visions of the Blessed Mother* (New York: Ballantine, 1995).

5 Louis-Marie Grignion de Montfort, *True Devotion to Mary* (edited by the Fathers of the Company of Mary, translated by F.W. Faber, 1941 (reprinted, Rockford, Ill.: Tan, 1985).

6 J. I. Pelletier, *Our Lady Comes to Garabandal* (Worcester, Mass.: Assumption, 1971).

7 R. Grant, "The Author Who Saw Jesus," in *Venture Inward* (Virginia Beach: ARE Press, March 1995).

8 G. S. Sparrow, *I Am with You Always: True Stories of Encounters with Jesus* (New York: Bantam, 1995.)

9 E. Shillebeeckx and C. Halkes, Mary—*Yesterday, Today, Tomorrow* (New York: Crossroad, 1993).

10 R. Faricy and L. Rooney, *Our Lady Comes to Scottsdale* (Medford, Ohio: Riehle Foundation, 1991).

11 R. Faricy, Foreword to J. T. Connell, *Meetings with Mary.*

12 J. I. Pelletier, *Mary Our Mother—Notes on Garabandal* (Worcester, Mass.: Assumption, 1972).

13 C. S. Lewis, *Letters to Malcolm: Chiefly on Prayer* (New York: Harcourt, Brace and World, 1963).

14 M. O'Carroll, *Theotokos—A Theological Encyclopedia of the Blessed Virgin Mary* (Wilmington: Michael Glazier, 1982).

15 A. C. Emmerich, *The Life of the Blessed Virgin Mary—From the Visions of Anne Catherine Emmerich* (Rockford, Illinois: Tan Books, 1970).

16 In the Introduction, Chapter Three, and Chapter Six.

17 R. Bucke, *Cosmic Consciousness* (New York: E. P. Dutton & Co., 1969, orig. 1901).

18 R. Wilhelm, *The Secret of the Golden Flower: A Chinese Book of Life,* translated and explained by Richard Wilhelm, with a commentary by C. G. Jung; translated from the German by Cary F. Baynes (San Diego: Harcourt Brace Jovanovich, 1961).

19 R. Laurentin, *Our Lord and Our Lady in Scottsdale* (Milford, Ohio: Faith Publishing, 1992), p. 25.

20 D. Blackbourn, *Marpingen—Apparitions of the Virgin Mary in a Nineteenth-Century German Village* (New York: Knopf, 1995).

21 J. Beevers, *The Sun Her Mantle* (Westminster, Md.: Newman Press, 1954).

22 J.I. Pelletier, *Our Lady Comes to Garabandal.*

23 Lama A. Govinda, *The Way of the White Clouds—A Buddhist Pilgrim in Tibet* (London: Hutchinson and Co., 1966).

24 A. M. Hancock, *Wake Up America.* (Norfolk: Hampton Roads, 1993).

25 Rev. Albert J. M. Shamon, *The Power of the Rosary,* (Medford, Ohio: Riehle Foundation, 1990), pp. 29–30.

26 A novena is a prayer dedicated to Mary or a particular saint that is done on a regular basis in order to obtain some healing or blessing.

27 L. Carroll, *Alice in Wonderland,* edited by Donald Gray (New York: Norton, 1992).

28 C. S. Lewis, *Letters to Malcolm.*

29 A rosary ring is an abbreviated form of the complete rosary that one can wear. The ring has ten raised knobs or "rosebuds" and one small cross on its outside surface, assisting the wearer in counting off ten Hail Marys before contemplating one of the Mysteries of the rosary.

[30] J. I. Pelletier, *Our Lady Comes to Garabandal.*

[31] E. Revillout in E. W. Budge, *Coptic Apocrypha in the Dialect of Upper Egypt* (London, 1913).

[32] E. Shillebeeckx and C. Halkes, *Mary.*

[33] We often think of the word *passion* as referring to love or lust, but it also means "being acted upon by external forces or fate." When it is used to describes Jesus' final days, therefore, it has more to do with *submitting fully* to the unfoldment of events that brought his life to fulfillment, however tragically. So, at the end of his life, Jesus mirrors Mary's responsiveness in that he "lets it be done unto him" so that good can be served.

[34] B. J. Eadie and C. Taylor, *Embraced by the Light* (Placerville, Ca.: Gold Leaf Press, 1992).

[35] An international lay movement founded in 1993 by Dr. Mark Miravalle, a professor of theology at Franciscan University of Steubenville, is urging the church to declare Mary as "Coredemtrix," "Mediatrix of grace," and "Advocate for the People of God." This proposed change in church dogma has gathered over four million signatures in petition, and enjoys the support of the late Mother Teresa, as well as over 40 cardinals and 480 bishops. It would reflect the beliefs of the faithful for centuries, and the practices of the church, but would confirm these beliefs in formal doctrine. The term *coredemtrix* implies that Christ has a partner in the redemptive process, but it does not imply that Mary is also "redeemer."

[36] J. Beevers, *The Sun Her Mantle.*

[37] C. S. Lewis, *Mere Christianity* (New York: Macmillan, 1952).

[38] A. C. Emmerich, *The Life of the Blessed Virgin Mary.*

[39] Donovan, Colin B., S.T.L., Homepage of Eternal Word Television Network: Global Catholic Network, http://www.ewtn.com/index.htm, under FAQs.

[40] C. S. Lewis, *Mere Christianity.*

[41] Actually, this is not entirely possible from the standpoint of the Catholic dogma of the Immaculate Conception (1854), which declared that Mary was conceived without the stain of original sin. This dogma, by implication, forever sets her apart from us. But for Protestants, who may not subscribe to this dogma, Mary remains one of us, and therefore an example of what we can do.

[42] M. Warner, *Alone of All Her Sex* (New York: Knopf, 1976).

[43] Maria Esperanza is the principal visionary of a series of Marian apparitions in Betania, Venezuela. For more information, see J. Connell's Meetings with Mary.

[44] D.C., or Dorothy Cox (name provided by consent), has published a booklet of Mary's messages, titled From My Immaculate Heart, available by e-mailing her at dotcox@nexicom.net, or writing to her at 584 Hopkins Ave., Petersborough, Ontario, Canada K9H 2S1.

[45] C. S. Lewis, *That Hideous Strength: A Fairy Tale for Adults* (New York: Scribner, 1946).

[46] Rachel is a massage therapist and considers her calling to be a healer.

[47] Rachel is referring to me.

[48] J. M. Haffert, *The Meaning of Akita* (Asbury, N. J.: 101 Foundation, 1989).

[49] M. O'Carroll, *Theotokos.*

[50] M. O'Carroll, ibid.

[51] J. I. Pelletier, *God Speaks at Garabandal—The Message of Garabandal with a Summary and Picture Story of the Apparitions* (Worcester, Mass.: Assumption, 1970).

[52] C. G. Jung, *The Collected Works of C. G. Jung,* vol. 9, part 1. (Princeton: Princeton University Press, 1969), p. 357.

[53] Matthew 12:48–50, John 19:26–27, John 21:15–17.

Postscript

THE PURPOSE OF
Sacred Encounters

IT HAS BEEN TWELVE YEARS SINCE I BEGAN A formal study of sacred encounters, but my interest in spiritual experiences began long before that—when I was a freshman at the University of Texas in 1970. It was then that I had my first encounter with the holy light in the midst of an unusual dream.

In this dream, I was walking home from my college classes, carrying my books. For some reason, I realized that I was dreaming. I stopped to look at my hands and my body, noting the vividness of every aspect of my experience. It seemed not only real, but more real than any waking experience. I concluded that my physical body was sleeping, but that I was nonetheless fully awake. Marveling at this paradox, I walked up to large black double doors, reached for ornate brass handles, and pulled open the doors. As soon as the doors parted, bright white light streamed through and filled my vision.

The sense of love and purpose was staggering as I felt the light course through my body with an authority that was at once undeniable and comforting. I felt I had come home, once and for all.

The interior seemed to be a small chapel, with large vertical windows looking out onto barren land. I walked about asking myself what it all meant. I thought that someone would surely appear at any moment to tell me why this was happening. At one point, I carried a crystal wand, at the top of which a spinning crystal circlet was hovering. The light passed through the crystal and was exquisitely beautiful.

While the room remained full of light, no one came to me. Alone in an empty room, I had no one to explain the sense of tremendous love and purpose that accompanied the radiance.

After having other experiences of the light and several encounters with Jesus and Mary, I thought that such experiences would increase in frequency. However, they began to occur less often than before. I wondered if perhaps I was "falling from grace," and no longer merited the gift of their presence. Even though I continued to meditate and pray about an hour every day, and I hoped that this spiritual practice would catalyze more spiritual experiences, the trend was clearly in the other direction. Eventually, it seemed, I was "on my own"—bereft of the spiritual sustenance that these encounters had brought me.

I thought that something was wrong, but I was simply looking for God in the wrong place.

When we consider the historic apparitions of Mary, we can see a similar pattern in which the Blessed Mother manifests to the visionaries for a period of time, and then ceases to appear. In the case of Medjugorje, we are told that her manifestations will cease once each visionary has received the full complement of her teachings. We can sense that Mary's purpose is not only to serve as an oracle for the faithful, but to conceive a new life in those that can receive her messages.

Some of the well-known visionaries, such as Bernadette of Lourdes, go on to give their lives to God in traditional ways. Others, such as Conchita of Garabandal, feel impelled to marry and to carry Mary's message into everyday life. Regardless, the end of the external manifestation coincides with a development within the visionary, in which spiritual communion and direction becomes a private, interior process. Some of the visionaries have even expressed relief that the apparitional stage is over and the interior communion has begun. For example, Conchita once said: "I prefer the locution to the apparitions, because in the locution I have her within me. . . . Oh, what happiness when I have the Blessed Virgin within me. . . . I prefer to have Jesus in me. . . . Here is the prayer I say to Jesus: 'Oh, my Jesus! Ay, Jesus mio!'"

Mary's external manifestations have permitted countless seekers to draw close to her essence and to experience more directly the purpose that God has in store for us. Even after she has ceased appearing, pilgrims continue to derive inspiration and healing from merely visiting the apparitional sites. But any phenomenal manifestation of Spirit always runs the risk of deepening our dependency on such things. It is clear that the apparitional stage must come to an end so that a more private, interior relationship can begin—one that can sustain the seeker through his or her lifetime in the absence of external signs and phenomena.

Of course, there is never any proof that such visions or apparitions have fulfilled their purpose in us. Perhaps we would have become the same persons anyway. All I can say is that I *feel* like a different person. When I recall the light, and the presence of Jesus and Mary, it is as though they are with me even now—not merely as memories, but as a perpetual interior presence. While we may grieve the disappearance of those who have anointed us with their love, we can also take heart that they now live within us, as a constant interior-felt presence that informs our choices, adds luster to our everyday duties, and overshadows us with a subtle charisma that others can feel and benefit from.

And so the question I think we need to ask is not, "How many visions have I had?" but "Do I feel God's presence within me?" If we can say yes, then the purpose of the apparitions—and of all sacred encounters—is being fulfilled in our lives.

G. Scott Sparrow, Ed. D., is a spiritual mentor, psycho-therapist, and writer who has published two books on Jesus and Mary. He received his bachelor's degree in psychology from the University of Texas at Austin, his master's degree in psychology from West Georgia College, and his doctorate in coun-seling from the College of William and Mary. His master's thesis and doctoral dissertation both focused on the phenomenon of "lucid dreaming," the experience of becoming aware that one is dreaming during the dream.

Dr. Sparrow has maintained a private practice in professional counseling for twenty years. He has lectured and taught courses across the United States on such topics as meditation, mystical experiences, and advanced dream work methods. He and his wife Kathy have three children and live in Arroyo City, Texas, where together they own the Kingfisher Inn and Guide Service, the only year-round fly fishing lodge on the Texas coast. They treasure the closeness to nature that their lifestyle affords them and consider it a spiritual calling to help people come into harmony with themselves in this remote, natural setting. Scott is a FFF-certified fly casting instructor and guides clients in the waters of the lower Laguna Madre.